Air Raid—
Pearl Harbor!

THEODORE TAYLOR

Air Raid—
Pearl Harbor!

THE STORY OF
DECEMBER 7, 1941

Gulliver Books
Harcourt, Inc.

SAN DIEGO   NEW YORK   LONDON

First published simultaneously by
Fitzhenry & Whiteside Limited, Toronto and
Thomas Y. Crowell Company, New York

First Gulliver Books paperbacks edition 2001
www.harcourt.com

Gulliver Books is a trademark of Harcourt, Inc., registered in
the United States of America and/or other jurisdictions.

Library of Congress Cataloging-in-Publication Data
Taylor, Theodore, 1921–
Air raid—Pearl Harbor!: the story of
December 7, 1941/by Theodore Taylor.
p. cm.—(Great Episodes)
Originally published: New York: Crowell, 1971.
Includes biographical references.
Summary: Examines from both the American and Japanese points of view
the political and military events leading up to the attack on Pearl Harbor.
1. Pearl Harbor (Hawaii), Attack on, 1941—Juvenile literature.
[1. Pearl Harbor (Hawaii), Attack on, 1941. 2. World War, 1939-1945
Causes. 3. Japan—Foreign relations—United States. 4. United States—
Foreign relations—Japan.] I. Title II. Series D767.92T39 2001
940.54′26—dc21 2001024185
ISBN 0-15-216421-9

Text set in AGaramond
Designed by Cathy Riggs

G I K J H F

Printed in the United States of America

To Christopher Robin, my grandson,
with a hope for peace during his lifetime

CONTENTS

1. The Spy Ship   1

2. The Purple Machine   17

3. The Submarines Sail   36

4. The Ships Sail   53

5. "Execute the Winds" Message   64

6. This Means War   78

7. Last Day of Peace: Honolulu   91

8. What Did "One O'Clock" Mean?   99

9. "Depth-Bombed Sub"   106

10. Attack! Attack! Attack!   120

11. This Is No Drill!   134

12. The *Arizona* Dies   145

13. The Second Wave   153

14. "A Date Which Will Live in Infamy"   164

15. The Heroes and the Scapegoats   172

*Key Figures in the Story
of Pearl Harbor*   185

Bibliography   187

Author's Note   191

Air Raid—
Pearl Harbor!

1

The Spy Ship

A JAPANESE LINER, the *Taiyo Maru,* steered into Honolulu harbor at 8:30 A.M. on November 1, 1941, moving slowly toward pier eight, near the famed Aloha Tower, a waterfront landmark, awaiting tugboat assistance.

The *Taiyo Maru* looked weather-beaten, as if she'd sailed rough North Pacific seas. Streaks of rust made ugly blotches on her hull. Most ships from Nippon came in spotless. They glistened. So, immediately, people on shore knew there was something strange about her.

According to a story in the previous day's *Honolulu Advertiser,* the *Taiyo Maru* might well be the last Japanese ship to visit the Hawaiian Islands for a very long time. Possibly, this was a *sayonara* voyage, a good-bye voyage.

Usually when a passenger ship was warped to the docks, a great celebration started up. Hula girls in grass skirts danced amid a throng of happy greeters, and the Royal Hawaiian Band filled the warm, moist air with music. Flower leis of carnations or pikake waited draped over many arms, ready to be flung around the newcomers' necks.

But this morning the greeters were almost ominously quiet; no pretty hula girls with swaying hips, no booming band in splendid uniforms. The people on the dock simply stared at the ship. The atmosphere was somber, though returning passengers crowded the *Taiyo Maru's* decks waving to friends and relatives ashore.

Until recently, Japanese ships had often called at the port, discharging passengers and cargo, taking on sugarcane products or pineapples for the voyage home. For years, Hawaiians had welcomed ships flying the white Japanese flag with the red ball, or rising sun, in the center. Many Japanese had emigrated to these islands, and they now thought of themselves as true and loyal Americans.

Once ruled by kings and queens, the Hawaiian Islands were annexed by the United States in 1898 and formally became an American territory in 1900. The first Japanese had emigrated fifteen years before that date. Most of them knew no other home. In the past eight months, however, serious political trouble had been developing between America and Japan.

No longer would ships like the *Taiyo Maru* be permitted to visit U.S. ports. And, naturally, Japan would not permit American-flagged vessels to call at her ports. The two nations had broken off trade relations.

Therefore, the story in the *Honolulu Advertiser* was quite correct. Chartered to bring stranded passengers home from Tokyo, she would take Japanese—those who wanted to go, or those who had been ordered to leave—back with her. She symbolized the end of friendly relations between the two nations. That's why the ship didn't receive the usual happy greeting on pier eight.

By shortly after nine o'clock she was tied up, and customs and immigration procedures began. Immigration authorities collected the passengers' entry papers, and customs agents handled clearance of any items purchased overseas. Secretly mixed in with them on this day, however, were agents of the Federal Bureau of Investigation and members of Army Intelligence Unit G-2.

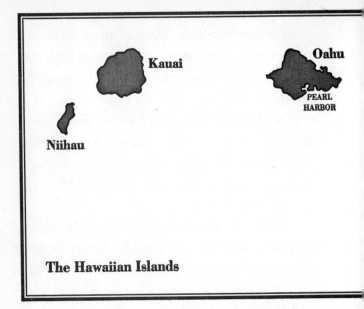

The Hawaiian Islands

The *Taiyo Maru* was of particular interest because Americans suspected the Japanese government might try to insert a spy into the islands on this final visit. The officials watched closely and listened as passports were examined and baggage was inspected.

After some hours, the *Taiyo Maru* was cleared. No documents or articles linking her to subversive activities were discovered; the passenger and crew lists seemed to be in good order. The immigration

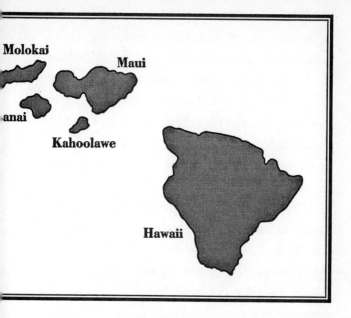

Molokai

Maui

anai

Kahoolawe

Hawaii

and customs authorities finally departed, and with them the suspicious FBI and G-2 representatives.

But as these officials left pier eight, at least four Japanese on board the liner breathed deep sighs of relief. They appeared on the crew list as members of the steward's department—personnel of the ship's crew who acted as waiters and food handlers, broom wielders and bed makers. Actually, the quartet were officers of the Imperial Japanese Navy.

Two of them were submarine experts. The other two—Lieutenant Commander Suguru Suzuki and Lieutenant Commander Toshihide Maejima—were experts in air operations and in surface ship operations. All had good reason to be relieved. On this voyage they were spies. For all of them, the trip from Japan had been tense. They'd spent endless hours just looking out to sea and scanning the bleak skies.

Others in the crew wondered why this silent foursome had been so interested in the skies and sea. In fact, almost everyone aboard the *Taiyo Maru* was puzzled by her route to Oahu, the main island. She took the lonely North Pacific passage between Midway Island and the icy Aleutians, one that frequently encountered heavy weather at this time of year. It was a very unusual course for a passenger ship to follow.

Suzuki and Maejima knew why that course had been chosen: The Japanese navy had ordered the *Taiyo Maru* to sail that northerly route, and the four masquerading stewards were under orders to watch for ships and aircraft on this desolate sea path to Honolulu. Now they could report to Tokyo that they didn't see a single vessel, not even a far-ranging fisherman; not once did they spot an aircraft in the gray, scudding skies.

To naval operations planners in Japan, including Admiral Isoroku Yamamoto, this was good news indeed. Yamamoto, commander in chief of the Combined Fleet of the Imperial Japanese Navy, was planning to attack the naval base at Honolulu's Pearl Harbor. He might well sail his ships along the little-traveled northern route.

Spread out in the middle of the blue-green Pacific Ocean were the eight lovely, tranquil, windswept islands. From little Niihau, the westernmost, to the big island of Hawaii, nearest the U.S. mainland, peace and contentment reigned.

Wars raged far away in Europe and China, and Hawaiians heard occasional echoes of the fighting, but in the islands people always listened more to wind songs in the palm and flame trees. By warm day and velvet night, the distant sounds and threats of war were often lost to moonlight and tumbling clouds.

Of course the people of heavily populated Oahu, the island on which the city of Honolulu is located, did have daily reminders of a troubled world. They saw the sprawling naval base at Pearl

Harbor, and the warships that were constantly clustered there. They heard the buzzing planes fly in and out of the Army Air Corps base at Hickam Field.

Many also knew that, of late, gun emplacements had been spotted around the island, and there was talk of some type of secret electronic device up in the hills. The mysterious device was set up on wheels and had a huge antenna that turned.

But they weren't worried. They believed the ships, the planes, the guns, and that mysterious electronic thing on wheels were there simply to preserve peace. What's more, they thought, no one would dare to attack the isles when all this equipment was ready on Oahu.

The residents also knew that there was an even greater weapon that was no secret at all. It was as old as the islands themselves, as old as the Polynesian warriors with their canoes and their knowledge of the seas and winds. It was distance.

Hawaii was thousands of miles from the German dictator, Adolf Hitler, and his dreams of Nazi domination of Europe if not the world. On September 1, 1939, his armies had moved against Poland, causing England and France to declare war against Germany three days later. The Allies also declared war against his partner Italy, led by dictator Benito Mussolini.

Already France had been defeated. Belgium, the Netherlands, Norway, Denmark, and tiny Luxembourg had also surrendered. England was still fighting desperately, supported by her allies— Canada, Australia, New Zealand, and South Africa. Hitler, whom the Allies now believed to be a madman, had attacked Russia in June of 1940.

Yet those bitter battles being fought all over Europe, and even on the desert sands of North Africa, seemed far removed from Hawaii. Japan, with her strong new navy, was much closer. Even so, almost four thousand miles separated Tokyo from Honolulu.

Besides, Japan was busy fighting China. Since 1931 she'd been sending troops to fight the Chinese. Japan was determined to expand her empire in Asia.

Distance, however, still made the people of the Hawaiian Islands feel safe from death and destruction, no matter what was taking place in Europe or Asia.

THE NEXT MORNING, November 2, was warm and sunpatched as the crew of the *Taiyo Maru* disembarked for a shore visit. One of the first men to go down the gangway was Suzuki. He took a taxi from pier eight to the Japanese consulate on Nuuanu Avenue, a short ride. Five buildings were enclosed in the consulate's compound, and in one resided the Honorable Nagao Kita, consul general. A veteran diplomat and a man who knew quite a bit about sensitive intelligence work, Kita had been alerted from Tokyo by cable that he would be paid a visit by one of the "stewards" from the *Taiyo Maru.*

He could only guess as to the exact purpose of Suzuki's morning call; but considering recent requests for information from Tokyo and a previous visit by one of Japan's top naval intelligence operators, it was hardly a difficult guess. The visit had something to do with Pearl Harbor.

The two men talked awhile, and then Suzuki handed Kita a piece of rice paper. On it, in meticulous Japanese script, were ninety-seven questions about the naval base and other military installations on the island of Oahu.

The naval base at Pearl Harbor was headquarters for two-thirds of the 102 major fighting ships of the U.S. Pacific Fleet. Together with the Atlantic Fleet, composed of 114 major fighting ships, the vessels represented America's total sea defense force.

Japanese naval experts knew Pearl Harbor was the key to American sea power in the Pacific. Here the ships were repaired, refueled, and stocked with ammunition. Pearl Harbor provided a base from which to conduct training exercises. Should the Americans happen to lose this vital military port, they might not be able to defend their interests in the Pacific.

Also on Oahu were the American Army Air Corps fields, Hickam and Wheeler; the navy seaplane base at Kaneohe; the Marine Corps air station at Ewa; and another navy field on Ford Island. Army troops were scattered all over the island. Oahu was truly an island fortress in the middle of the Pacific.

Suzuki said that Tokyo officials demanded immediate answers to their questions about Oahu. Soon Commander Suzuki left Kita to the task and returned to the ship at pier eight.

Kita then summoned a young man known to the Americans as Tadashi Morimura. He was listed in U.S. State Department records and in immigration records under that name, his occupation described as "apprentice consul." But

11

Morimura had far more in common with Commander Suzuki than he did with Nagao Kita's other apprentices. His true name was Takeo Yoshikawa, and he was an ensign in the Imperial Navy. He spoke excellent English.

Since March, Yoshikawa had been extremely busy—but not with consular affairs. He, too, was a spy, and he had been collecting information about the American navy, army, and Marine Corps.

Twenty-eight years old, possessed of a ready smile, taller and heavier than most Japanese, Yoshikawa made friends on Oahu quickly. They ranged from waitresses and schoolteachers to members of the Japanese community. He was seldom around the consulate, spending most of his time roaming over Oahu. Occasionally he visited the other islands.

He often went sight-seeing, and he had even flown over Pearl Harbor, collecting valuable information while passing as a simple tourist. Sometimes he talked to sailors and soldiers. He was always careful not to ask too many questions. The most daring thing he'd done was to use his small camera on a plane ride over the naval base.

Most of Yoshikawa's activities, but not his aerial camera work, were known to American counterintelligence agents. They were considered normal and routine, part of the usual consular work. Every diplomatic outpost in any country gathered information, including military data. So they allowed Yoshikawa's sight-seeing to continue.

Although FBI and army intelligence experts knew Nagao Kita had many part-time agents in his huge staff of assistants, spread out around all the islands, they did not suspect young Morimura, the engaging apprentice consul. Even the other members of Kita's staff at the compound didn't know he was a spy. To them, he was a brash upstart and not very bright.

But he was much wiser than he looked or acted. He watched the warships parade in and out of Pearl Harbor, noting names and types, and arrival and departure times. He was most interested in the battleships and in the two huge aircraft carriers, *Enterprise* and *Lexington*. So he was well prepared to answer the questions submitted by Suzuki.

He went over the list with Kita. Easily the most important question was "On what day would most of the ships be in Pearl Harbor?" His answer was quick and definite. A Sunday! Any Sunday!

From his months of patient observation, Ensign Yoshikawa knew that the ships of the Pacific Fleet usually steamed back to port for the weekends after training exercises off the island. Sunday was a religious day of rest for most Americans. And there was something else about Sunday— many of the off-duty officers and chiefs would be ashore. None of the ships would be fully manned.

Yoshikawa managed to answer most of the questions on the crumpled piece of rice paper, not really aware that he was helping to seal the fate of two nations that November 2 on Nuuanu Avenue.

In the leisure of the afternoon, Consul General Kita was driven from the compound to pier eight. He, too, had little real knowledge of the momentous decisions that were being made in Tokyo. At the moment he was just a courier, carrying out instructions.

Kita boarded the *Taiyo Maru* with an official-looking package under his arm. The ship was again being watched by American intelligence agents, but it was not unusual for the consul general to visit his nation's vessels while they were in port, especially one like the chartered liner. Many legitimate matters of business required attention.

Kita located Commanders Suzuki and Maejima, and they went into a stateroom well away from the crew's prying eyes and ears. They locked the door. Then Kita opened his package, and the contents were spread out. They included maps of Pearl Harbor and of the military airfields, as well as sketches and aerial photographs. The documents, of course, represented the patient work of Vice-Consul Morimura.

By nightfall, Suzuki and Maejima had accomplished most of their assigned mission. But the *Taiyo Maru* would be in port for two more days before she set sail again for Japan. So they spent part of each remaining day ashore and picked up other information. It was quite easy, as Yoshikawa had learned before them.

Fine souvenir picture postcard sets were available in the Waikiki shops, the kinds of sets that sailors often sent home to girlfriends and relatives. They contained photographic reproductions of some of the largest ships in the Pacific Fleet. One postcard featured an exceptional view of Battleship Row, the mooring area by Ford Island where the big capital ships tied up on weekends.

Suzuki, the aviator, was particularly delighted with that photograph. It was quite the best aerial view of Pearl Harbor he'd ever seen. It would delight the operational planners in Japan, too, should they decide to go ahead with an air raid. Reproductions of this view might also be excellent for taping to the instrument panels of the aircraft.

In late afternoon on November 5, the Royal Hawaiian Band, which had been absent for the *Taiyo Maru*'s arrival, began to play on pier eight. The *Taiyo Maru* was preparing to depart, and strains of "Aloha Oe," that happy and yet sad song, echoed along the waterfront.

But not until after dark—about 7:30 P.M.— did the liner finally slip away and stand out to sea. Four hundred and forty-eight returning passengers were aboard, most of them Japanese citizens.

For the four stewards, especially Commanders Suzuki and Maejima, the voyage had been highly successful.

2

The Purple Machine

ACROSS AN EXPANSE of ocean and over a continent, a top secret machine known only as "Purple" was clacking away in Washington, D.C.

Purple was a code breaker consisting of what appeared to be two separate teletype machines. It looked somewhat like the usual wire machines that were found in every newspaper office at the time. Purple broke the codes of secret diplomatic messages from Japan, giving government workers a way to decipher the messages.

Intelligence and spying activities between nations were never a one-way street. While Yoshikawa and the men on the *Taiyo Maru* carried out their mission for Japan, Purple was working for the United States against Japan. As a matter of security, most nations relayed all their important

messages by code. Most also made an effort to break the codes of other nations and learn the information conveyed.

In August 1940, after many months of brilliant work by cryptology experts, Purple finally succeeded in breaking the Japanese diplomatic

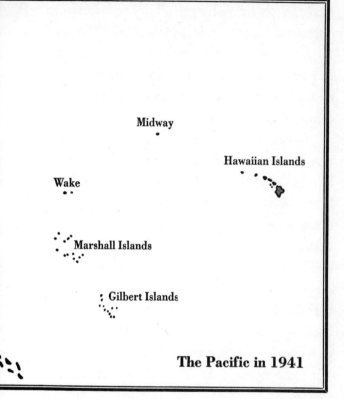

Midway

Hawaiian Islands

Wake

Marshall Islands

Gilbert Islands

The Pacific in 1941

code. Since that time, the United States had an ear in on all the diplomatic messages transmitted between Tokyo and Japanese officials stationed in America. Powerful listening posts, manned by expert radio operators, were placed around the country and out on Pacific islands. They "listened" to the Japanese transmissions around the clock and relayed them to Washington. The entire top secret operation that involved Purple was called "Magic."

Some of the messages over the past months had been alarming. Japan, incredibly, seemed to be readying for a war that went beyond her recent moves in China.

President Franklin D. Roosevelt, Secretary of State Cordell Hull, Secretary of War Henry Stimson, and Secretary of the Navy Frank Knox knew of the Magic operation and had access to the messages. They couldn't keep possession of them, not even file copies, for fear that unauthorized people might see them. To trained eyes, the mere sight of the decoded messages would reveal that the United States had broken the Japanese code—a discovery that would lead the Japanese to invent a new code to frustrate the U.S.

Some of the top-ranking military officers, such as Army Chief of Staff General George C. Marshall and Chief of Naval Operations Admiral Harold Stark, were also aware of Purple's output. But Purple was of such a highly secret nature that few besides these key officials had any knowledge of the machine's existence. The military leaders in Hawaii, Admiral Husband Kimmel, Commander in chief, Pacific (CINCPAC), and Lieutenant General Walter Short, the army's Hawaiian chief, had never even heard of it, nor did they realize that the United States was following every diplomatic maneuver Japan made.

Several of the closely guarded decoding machines were in Washington, administered by Navy Intelligence and by the army's G-2. After the messages were decoded and translated, they were carried to the White House, the State Department, and other privileged offices in locked leather pouches. The security chain around these documents was the tightest in the entire government.

However, long before these crucial days of early November 1941, President Roosevelt had thought about the possibility of conflict with the small—but very strong—Asian nation. As early as 1933, he'd mentioned it to Harry Hopkins, his longtime friend and confidant, in private conversation.

Then, the previous January, Roosevelt wrote to the American ambassador in Tokyo, Joseph C. Grew:

> I believe that the fundamental proposition is that we must recognize that the

hostilities in Europe, in Africa, and in Asia are all parts of a *single world conflict.* We must, consequently, recognize that our interests are menaced both in Europe, and in the Far East. . . .

Six days later, Grew wrote to the State Department:

A member of the embassy was told by my Peruvian colleague that from many quarters, including a Japanese one, he had heard that a surprise attack on Pearl Harbor was planned by the Japanese military forces, in case of "trouble" between Japan and the United States; that the attack would involve the use of all Japanese military forces. . . .

But as the year ebbed out, the people on the U.S. mainland, as well as those in Hawaii, still thought of Japan as a strange, backward place, a country so very far away that it could not possibly be considered an enemy. If war did come to America, they thought, it would certainly be with that old opponent Germany.

Most Americans thought of the Japanese as people who made cheap toys and had large front teeth and bad eyesight. Supposedly, they couldn't pronounce *l*'s, and they said "prease" instead of "please." Japan was thought to be a silly, funny place full of kimonos and paper houses, a place where people copied merchandise made in the United States or England and always took off their wooden shoes before entering a home.

Only a few civilians, and not even many military personnel, knew that Japan had a larger and more modern navy than did the United States; swift, new aircraft carriers; and, in some instances, superior planes and superior pilots. In reality, then, for a long time, "quaint" Japan, with its brooding inferiority complex, had been one of the most misunderstood nations on earth.

Being misunderstood, and underrated militarily, she was at this point very dangerous.

Many things had occurred since Japan moved troops into Manchuria in 1931—the result of an incident that Japan herself provoked. In 1937 she unleashed her armies for full-scale war with China. That same year, she bombed and sank the U.S. gunboat *Panay* in Chinese waters.

But these events had been largely ignored by most Americans. A vast segment of the population wanted to keep America isolated from troubles in the Far East and in Europe. They did not want war with *either* Japan or Germany. Even if England was conquered, they wanted to remain aloof.

Yet, in the face of that political opposition, President Roosevelt paved the way to supply England with munitions and old destroyers. And he wanted to do even more to help defend the British.

The Far East was quite another matter. It truly seemed so remote to most Americans that they tended to look the other way despite the *Panay* incident, other gunnings of U.S. naval craft, and the murder and harassment of American missionaries.

Then there was President Roosevelt's campaign promise of 1940. He assured Americans that he would not commit their sons to fight in foreign lands.

Yet more and more it looked as though he would have to break his promise, give even more assistance to England, and eventually slide into war with Hitler's Germany. But, plainly, America was not equipped or in the political frame of mind to fight both Germany and Japan. So the Far East remained a secondary threat.

However, as a secondary threat, Japan in 1941 controlled vast territories within China and had its bases firmly established in French Indochina (an area that today includes the countries of Cambodia, Laos, and Vietnam). Japan was the most powerful nation in all Asia, and she was on the march.

Bulging with people spread over her four main islands of Honshu, Kyushu, Shikoku, and Hokkaido, as well as dozens of smaller islands, Japan needed raw materials to support her industry. She possessed relatively little of what she needed within her own boundaries. These could be gained from China, from French-dominated Indochina, and from the oil-and-rubber-rich Dutch East Indies (Indonesia). Holland's colonial empire included Java, Sumatra, and part of New Guinea. Japan also had her eyes on Malaya, Burma, the big island of Borneo, and even the Philippines.

But more than just a conquest of land and gain of raw materials drove her. The Japanese saw themselves as leaders of all Asia, spreading influence both politically and militarily. They also resented white domination of land and economy in

East Asia—domination by the British, French, and Dutch. They resented America's trade policies and her friendship with China.

These resentments were clearly evident even in 1938, when Prince Fumimaro Konoye, the prime minister, announced the concept of a "New Order" in East Asia, one in which Japan would lead the way not only in military and political affairs, but also in economic and cultural activities.

The old slogan *Hakko ichiu*, or "bringing the eight corners of the world under one roof," had been renewed. A majority of both political and military leaders advocated expansion, and they found most Japanese people also supported this policy. When millions of people are crammed together on small islands, it is relatively easy to convince them that they need more land.

The leaders also appealed to ancient and overwhelming Japanese national pride, and to the people's firm belief in their destiny. The leaders claimed they could bring great and lasting prosperity to all Asia. The citizens of Japan listened and agreed.

Foreign observers felt that Japan's greatest desire was to be a major power, *the* major power in Asia. It didn't matter that most Asian peoples preferred to rule themselves, whether they were Chinese, Malays, or Javanese. But the Japanese, foreign observers said, thought they knew what was best for all Asians.

Still another force was at work underneath these. Perhaps even more compelling than politics, this force was the samurai spirit, the spirit of the warrior. Japan was now being blindly guided by the ancient ways of the samurai, the ways of the old warlords.

Only one power stood in the warlords' way in the Far East and Pacific—the United States.

Japan knew America could not remain forever aloof and idle while Japan conquered China, Holland's territories in the East Indies, French Indochina, and British possessions, including Hong Kong and Singapore. The United States was friendly to all four nations. More than that, Japan's military expansion posed a direct threat to the Philippines, islands protected by the United States. It was quite evident by now that Japan wanted the Philippines as part of her so-called prosperity sphere.

Indirectly, Japan also threatened such U.S. mid-Pacific possessions as Midway, Guam, and Wake Islands. All three had defense significance.

Marines were stationed on Wake, and the island was a refueling stop for Pan-American clippers, the big flying boats, on their way to the Orient. Guam had been a naval refueling stop for years. Midway was the last defensive outpost before Hawaii.

Japan had bases in the Marshall Islands, the Gilberts, the Carolines, and the Marianas—possessions she gained after World War I—and these bases threatened America's stations. Guam, for instance, was less than a hundred miles from Saipan, a heavily fortified Japanese base in the Marianas. Wake was not too far from Japan's base of Kwajalein, in the Marshalls. So the United States had interests to protect beyond her commitments to allies.

Japan's leaders knew the "New Order" in Asia and its dreams of *Hakko ichiu,* world domination, could not succeed unless the United States stood aside or was defeated in battle.

Thus far, the United States had not used the force of her navy in Pacific or Chinese waters. She had been slowly increasing her military strength in the Philippines, and there were other signs that the nation was planning to face Japan squarely.

Up to this time, America had used only political weapons. In September 1940, she stopped selling Japan the scrap iron necessary to the war effort in China. In the same year, she banned the sale of oil to Japan. Without oil, Japan's war machine could not operate for long. In July, with England as partner, America froze all of Japan's assets in the United States, making it impossible for her to carry on any further trade with private businesses in the States and in England. These measures were all designed to force Japan to stop her warring in the Far East.

America demanded that Japan cease fighting with China, withdraw from Indochina, and pursue a peaceful course in the Far East.

So, by November 2, 1941, all but diplomatic relations between the United States and Japan had been severed. The two nations were still talking on high levels, but every other contact between them had been broken. They were enemies, but not yet at war.

Meanwhile, Japan made treaties with Nazi Germany and Italy, as partners in the European Axis, and she'd even forged a neutrality pact with Soviet Russia, now at war with her former ally Germany.

So the sides were sharply drawn up, politically

if not militarily—Germany, Italy, and Japan against England and the United States.

Yet few of Japan's leaders, except some high-ranking army officers, wanted open war with America. They wanted to achieve their objectives without war. Navy leaders, too, were generally against it. The highly regarded Admiral Yamamoto, who had served in America and was aware of its industrial might, spoke out against such a move. In fact, so outspoken was Yamamoto that it was feared he would be assassinated by Japanese army officers.

He gave a talk at Japan's naval academy, telling the young officer candidates:

Most people think the Americans love luxury, and that their culture is shallow and meaningless. It is a mistake to regard them as luxury-loving and weak. I have lived among them, and I can tell you they are a people full of the spirit of justice, fight, and adventure. What is more, their thinking is very advanced and scientific. Lindbergh's solo crossing of the Atlantic is the sort of valiant act typical of them—a typical American adventure, based on science. Do not forget, American industry is much more developed than ours. And un-like us, they have all the oil they want. Japan cannot beat America. Therefore, she should not even think of fighting America.

Words like these enraged many Japanese army officers, even though they knew that Yamamoto, having studied at Harvard and having been a naval attaché in Washington, was qualified to speak them.

As a result of army influence, the samurai spirit had grown steadily since 1937. Now General Hideki Tojo, minister of war, was one of the most powerful men in all Japan. Nicknamed "Kamisori," or "Razor Blade," Tojo seldom hid the fact that he believed war with America was inevitable.

Japan's Emperor Hirohito was a peaceful man, and by tradition he ruled Japan as a spiritual rather than a political leader. He didn't want war with any nation, and while he was often consulted and expressed his thoughts, he left the final decisions to his political leaders, who were more in touch with the global situation. Most of the time he was removed and aloof from the world, even from his own people. He lived behind the walls, moats, and manicured green gardens of the Imperial Palace in Tokyo.

Prince Konoye, who was Japan's prime minister until October 1941, was equally weak. He resigned his position rather than face the opposition of the army. He, too, was fearful of going to war with America. The new prime minister was none other than the so-called Kamisori—the tough, relentless "Razor Blade," General Hideki Tojo. He still held his old post of war minister and now, as prime minister, was also Japan's political leader. Without question he controlled Japan.

As November moved along, feverish day-and-night meetings were held in Tokyo. The participants decided to submit still more proposals and demands to the American government. If the demands were not met, then Japan's military forces would begin operations in early December.

These demands, known as Proposal A, included U.S. acceptance of Japanese army units remaining in North China, Mongolia, and Hainan for a "necessary period," and acceptance by the United States of a trade policy for China and the Pacific that would remove all economic bans and restrictions on Japan. In addition, Tojo wanted the United States to persuade China's leader, Generalissimo Chiang Kai-shek, to make peace with Japan.

The demands were harsh. The United States, in effect, had to sanction Japan's occupation of large areas of China and force Chiang Kai-shek to lay down his arms.

There was little reason to believe that America would accept Proposal A, and at almost the same time (since the military must plan well ahead of political and diplomatic discussions) Admiral Yamamoto issued a secret operations order.

Despite his continued opposition to attacking the United States, Yamamoto was carrying out his orders as commander in chief of the navy and as a professional military man. In fact, it was Yamamoto who conceived the plan to attack Pearl Harbor. Quite a while before this month of November, he said to Prime Minister Konoye, "If I am told to fight, regardless of the consequences, I will run wild for six months, or a year, but have no confidence for the second or third years..."

Yamamoto, with a long reputation within the Japanese navy as an excellent bridge player and winning gambler, was about to gamble in another game, one with very high stakes. He ordered Vice

Admiral Chuichi Nagumo, the man who would command the attack fleet, to have his ships at Tankan Bay by November 22 for refueling. They were to stand by for further orders.

Tankan Bay (also known as Hittokappu), in the Kuriles, then part of Japan, was a thousand miles north of Hokkaido, Japan's northernmost island. The big bay was an ideal place to assemble a secret battle force. Only a few fishermen lived along its rugged shores. The region was often hooded in mist and blanketed in snow.

The date of the attack on Pearl Harbor had been set for Sunday, December 7—which would be Monday, December 8, across the International Date Line, in Japan.

Yamamoto and his navy staff accepted Ensign Yoshikawa's advice and planned a Sunday raid. Actually, Yamamoto had already decided to raid on a Sunday, but he'd wanted affirmation before making final plans.

Daring as it was, the Pearl Harbor blow was to be just one part of an even larger plan. Almost simultaneously the Japanese would strike the Philippines, Malaya, Hong Kong, and Thailand. Then they would advance to the Dutch East Indies, and finally on to occupy Burma. Their goal was to have troops along the border of India within months.

They planned to smash the U.S. bases on Guam and Wake quickly, later to take Midway.

Viewed on paper, in geographical outline alone, it was a staggering plan of conquest, and the bombs destined to fall at Pearl Harbor would echo throughout Asia.

3

The Submarines Sail

BY THE END of the first week in November, Vice Admiral Nagumo's strike force of the First Air Fleet was being readied for the long voyage, even though it might not take place.

His floating airfields, the carriers—the launching platforms for his aircraft—were his own flagship, *Akagi*, and the ships *Kaga, Soryu, Hiryu, Zuikaku*, and *Shokaku*.

The aircraft carriers would sail as a group—a task force—and to protect them from surface attack and provide antiaircraft defense, Nagumo would have the battleships *Hiei* and *Kirishima*; two cruisers, *Tone* and *Chikuma*; and nine modern, fast destroyers.

The destroyers, especially, would need extra fuel on the trip, so oil tankers were going to accompany the task force to refuel it en route, a hazardous undertaking in heavy seas. As an added precaution, the ships would carry extra fuel drums, and already those drums were being stacked in Tankan Bay for transfer to the task force.

American ships are usually named for people, battles, states, cities, and sometimes rivers; submarines often take their names from fish. But it was typically Japanese that *Akagi* means "Red Castle," *Kaga* means "Increased Joy," and *Zuikaku* means "Happy Crane." One of the destroyers was named *Kasumi,* which means "Mist of Flowers." But, of course, samurais were also poets and wrote charming verse on paper screens, before plunging their swords into the enemy.

The man assigned the key role in the formulation of Admiral Yamamoto's plans for Pearl Harbor was Commander Minoru Genda, a rather small, wiry man with bright, burning eyes, a crack pilot as well as a strategist. After much study, he and the admiral drew up their plans, and they even played out a mock attack on a huge board at the Naval War College in Tokyo.

Genda supervised the selection and the training of the pilots. They had been practicing since September, not realizing in the early weeks the mission that was ahead of them. They bombed imaginary Hawaiian targets at Kagoshima Bay, on the island of Kyushu, and they made low-level torpedo runs with torpedoes that were designed specifically for use in the shallow waters of Pearl Harbor. Not until the first week in October did the pilots learn of the daring plan to smash the U.S. fleet.

Genda barely slept at all while he went over and over the plans to destroy Admiral Kimmel's ships and reduce America to a state of helplessness in the Pacific. On paper, Genda had 432 planes available on the six carriers. Of this number, 353 had been designated for the attack mission. The others were to be held either in reserve or for defensive air patrol over the task force after the strike aircraft were launched.

The attacking force of aircraft, to be sent off the carriers in two waves, would include 103 Nakajima torpedo bombers loaded with sixteen-inch converted naval shells. These planes would fly at a high level and drop their explosives on the ships or airfields below. There would be another 40 of the same type of aircraft with the shallow-water torpedoes slung beneath. They would come in low and drop the deadly "tin fish" at the battleships and carriers. Assigned were 131 Aichi-99 dive-bombers, along with 79 Mitsubishi-A6M2 fighter aircraft, to engage U.S. fighter planes and also strafe ground installations with machine-gun fire.

Lieutenant Commander Mitsuo Fuchida, an old friend of Genda's, and a fine and daring pilot, was to lead the first strike wave. Genda was principally responsible for his selection.

So all the elements were on paper, the pilots were trained, and the orders had been issued for assembly. No nation had ever begun a war with an attack from aircraft carriers, and the fleet now placed under command of Vice Admiral Nagumo was indeed formidable.

But beneath his brusque attitude, and behind his hard, cold eyes and sporty mustache, Nagumo was worried. Once the force sailed, he was responsible for both fighting with it and protecting it. He was not a gambler like Yamamoto. The nightmare of being discovered before the attack and losing his carriers was never far from his mind.

THERE WAS ALSO uneasiness in Washington, a feeling of uncertainty—but it was not of quite the same nature. On November 7, exactly thirty days before the attack date chosen by Yamamoto, President Roosevelt sat with his cabinet, asking for the latest information on the Japanese situation. He also asked for advice.

The distinguished, white-haired secretary of state, Cordell Hull, soft-spoken but tough as the hickory trees from his native Tennessee, said bluntly that the situation was serious. Japan might attack at any time. But all present thought an attack would come in the far reaches of the Pacific, perhaps to bases in Malaya or the Philippines. Not in Hawaii!

It would take considerable imagination to arrive at the island of Oahu as a place the enemy would strike, again simply because of its distance from Japan. And the key members of Roosevelt's cabinet were not particularly imaginative. Both Hull and Secretary of War Henry Stimson were aging and ailing. Roosevelt himself, partly crippled from infantile paralysis, was not in the best of health.

This same chill night along the Potomac, Japan's tall and scholarly ambassador to the United States, Admiral Kichisaburo Nomura, called on Hull to present his government's new Proposal A for peace in the Pacific. Informed by Purple's decoded messages, Hull already knew the terms that Nomura would present. But he pretended he was reading Proposal A for the first time.

He did not reject the proposal. He didn't offer encouragement that the United States would accept it, either. He was simply polite and attentive, hinting to Nomura that Japan could find ways to become Asia's "moral" leader without being aggressive and occupying other countries.

Then, at Nomura's request, Hull arranged a meeting with the president so the ambassador could personally present his government's request to the American head of state. This meeting took place November 10 at the White House, and Roosevelt's answer to Nomura was firm: *Japan can prove its desire for peace in Asia only by beginning to move its troops out of China and Indochina.*

Hull, present at the meeting between Nomura and Roosevelt, noted the look of dismay spreading over Nomura's face. The Japanese ambassador knew that Prime Minister Tojo would flatly refuse to withdraw troops. By late afternoon of November 10, Proposal A—never a true means to peace—was a useless document.

In fact, all of Nomura's sincere efforts were about to become quite useless. The admiral had no way of knowing it as he dejectedly left the White House, but already eleven of Japan's submarines were moving toward Hawaii. They'd slipped out of the big naval base at Yokosuka the day before and were now advancing to the north on a great-circle course to pass between Midway Island and the Aleutians. They were following almost the same route plied by the *Taiyo Maru.*

Another nine subs had sailed earlier. Five more would soon depart, these last carrying a particularly sinister weapon in the form of midget submarines manned by volunteers who had little hope of returning to the Land of the Rising Sun.

For some time Nomura had been disheartened. He had already asked to be relieved of his post. A naval officer by training, not a diplomat, Nomura had also requested help in the tense negotiations with Washington. In a few days another Japanese envoy, Saburo Kurusu, arrived to take up residency at the embassy. He was a veteran and skilled career diplomat, but in appearance and manner he was almost the opposite of lanky, friendly Admiral Nomura. To Cordell Hull, Kurusu immediately seemed deceitful. Hull did not trust him at all, and eventually some in

Washington were to suspect that Kurusu knew of the plan to strike Pearl Harbor well in advance.

The subs had sailed, and in light of that, Kurusu's knowledge of Tokyo's final move was of little importance. If, by any chance, Nomura and Kurusu were successful in further negotiations, the submarines could be recalled and the task force, not yet at Tankan Bay, would steam back to peaceful anchorages in the Inland Sea.

HAWAIIAN OFFICIALS also felt Washington's anxiety. But they were not worried enough to sound an alert or place military units on a war footing. The army commander, General Walter Short, was much more concerned about the possibility of sabotage than he was about armed attack. He worried that some of the more than 150,000 people of Japanese descent living in the islands might be more loyal to Tokyo than to their adopted land.

So Short went about stationing more guards at various installations and huddling his aircraft together at such fields as Hickam, Wheeler, and Bellows. Now sentries could patrol with greater ease and stay on guard to prevent sabotage in case war broke out elsewhere in the Pacific.

Admiral Husband Kimmel, a tall Kentuckian, a "spit and polish" officer, did not share General Short's fears of sabotage by Japanese living in Hawaii. He recognized the dangers, but as commander in chief of all naval forces in the Pacific, he was more worried about hostile actions far away. For instance, the Asiatic Fleet, a small and rather feeble force based in Manila, could be endangered.

On November 7, Kimmel's superior in Washington, Admiral Stark, wrote, "Things seem to be moving steadily toward a crisis in the Pacific. Just when it will break, no one can tell." Beginning in April, Kimmel had already received other such letters from Stark, but so far none contained a specific warning.

By November, however, Kimmel had stationed submarines off Wake and Midway Islands, the mid-Pacific bases, as sentinels, and in position to attack an approaching fleet. He added more marines to the small garrisons on Wake and Johnston Islands, and he placed certain warships in U.S. West Coast ports on a twelve-hour sailing notice in case of a sudden outbreak of hostilities.

Yet Kimmel had not appeared to be particularly worried about immediate surprise attack on his ships at Pearl Harbor, ships that he could see daily from his commander in chief's office at the submarine base.

However, the officer he had relieved, Admiral James Richardson, openly viewed Pearl Harbor as a "mousetrap," a harbor they couldn't get out of easily. Because of this, he'd pleaded with Washington to shift the main units of the fleet back to ports on the west coast of the United States. (Until the spring of 1940, the fleet had been based in California.)

The decision to base the fleet permanently at Pearl Harbor was made by President Roosevelt, who believed its proximity to Asia would act as a deterrent to Japanese aggression. Japan, naturally, viewed the decision as another sign of hostility by the Americans.

Richardson's open opposition to berthing the big ships at Pearl annoyed the president, and early in 1941, Roosevelt had replaced him with Kimmel.

So the battleships, ships that were still considered the strongest elements of the fleet by many, had their home in the harbor that Richardson likened to a mousetrap.

Of course, Pearl Harbor also docked aircraft

carriers, cruisers, destroyers, and submarines, along with supporting vessels such as repair ships, oilers, supply freighters, tugs, and small craft. At times the in-ship board—a type of bulletin board—of the Fourteenth Naval District, also headquartered at Pearl Harbor, indicated more than a hundred vessels at docks, moorings, and anchorages.

The battleships were the largest of the surface vessels. Their guns were capable of hurling tons of shells at an enemy. Barrels projected from their main turrets like fat telephone poles. The cruisers were smaller, often faster, versions of the battle-ships. The destroyers, still smaller, fired not only guns but torpedoes as well, and they were used to escort the larger vessels and to fight off enemy submarines.

The ships often sailed in task forces, units composed of all types of combatant ships. Essentially, task forces were floating gun platforms, and their basic mission was to destroy an enemy fleet.

Kimmel and Short both faced the same problem: too few men, and too much obsolete equipment. Short's soldiers were drilling with World War I weapons, and Kimmel did not have enough patrol aircraft to maintain a far-ranging search of the waters off Hawaii. Both the army and the navy suffered from a lack of funds, and only within the past two years had the United States made an effort to rebuild military defenses.

Perhaps even worse than the shortage of equipment—old and worn as it was—and worse than the lack of adequate manpower, was the lack of proper intelligence information from Washington. Headquarters for each of the military intelligence services were in the nation's capital, and they acted as collection stations for information. Experts in Washington analyzed the information received from various sources around the world, and then they supposedly channeled pertinent data back to field commanders.

By nature and by training, however, intelligence personnel usually cloaked their functions in heavy secrecy. Sometimes the secrecy was so jealously guarded that persons who needed to know a bit of vital information, simply in order to make a wise decision, found out that the information was forbidden to them. Even President Roosevelt was taken off the Magic distribution list for a period because it was feared there were information leaks in the White House.

Both Kimmel and Short were unknowingly caught in this web of supersecrecy. In the middle of November, they were still denied knowledge of Purple and Magic. And Purple, especially with the arrival of Kurusu, was working overtime to decode the many messages transmitted from Tokyo to Japanese stationed in America—and the messages sent back to Tokyo.

On November 13, Admiral Nomura cabled Foreign Minister Shigenori Togo in Tokyo to tell him that if Japan pressed on with the "southward venture," the movement toward Malaya and Siam, the United States would surely join England in fighting her. Nomura suggested that Tokyo "be patient for one or two months in order to get a clear view of the world situation."

The next day, Purple decoded Togo's answer: *The deadline for the solution of the negotiations has been set, and there will be no change. Press Washington for a favorable solution!*

As the message was read in the State Department, and eventually in the White House, there was little doubt in anyone's mind that a solid stalemate existed. As each day turned to night, the two nations had less to talk about, less room in which to make diplomatic moves.

Codes were curious, often chilling mixtures of words, and on November 19—as the Japanese submarines were progressing steadily across the Pacific, now trailed by five submarines with midget subs mounted in huge, waterproof steel tubes on their decks—another message from Tokyo to the Japanese embassy in Washington was intercepted. It was fed into Purple and came out:

1. East wind, rain (*Higashi no kaze ame*): In case of Japanese and United States relations failing.
2. North wind, cloudy (*Kitanokaze kumori*): In case of Japanese and Soviet Russian relations failing.
3. West wind, cloudy (*Nishi no kaze hare*): In case of Japanese and British relations failing.

This "winds" signal was to be transmitted at the end of the regular Tokyo weather broadcast; each sentence was to be repeated twice. When it was heard, those in charge of embassies and consulates in the countries concerned should immediately destroy all codes and other secret materials.

Read by personnel in both Navy Intelligence and the army's G-2, the message, soon to be known as the "Winds Execute" message, was interpreted by some to be a war warning.

Plainly, it established procedures to be used in case of extreme international emergencies. It was an ominous message. Yet neither Admiral Kimmel nor General Short in Hawaii, nor army commander General Douglas MacArthur in the Philippines, was notified of its existence. To tell them would probably mean revealing the existence of Purple and the fact that the Japanese code had been broken, and government officials were still afraid of security leaks.

Five days later, Admiral Stark did send a top secret dispatch to Admiral Kimmel at Pearl Harbor, and to Admiral Hart in Manila:

> Chances of a favorable outcome of negotiations with Japan very doubtful. This situation coupled with statements of Japanese government and movements of their naval and military forces indicate in our opinion that a surprise move in any direction including attack on Philippines or Guam is a possibility. Chief of Staff [General George C. Marshall] has seen this dispatch, concurs and requests action addresses to inform senior Army officers their areas. Utmost secrecy in order not

to complicate an already tense situation or precipitate Japanese action.

Kimmel duly informed General Short, whose headquarters were at Fort Shafter, a serene old army post not too far from Pearl Harbor, and Hart passed the message to General MacArthur in Manila.

But already time was running out. Nagumo's ships were at Tankan Bay. Singly, doubly, routinely, they had sailed from the Inland Sea, from Kure, and from Yokosuka. They were now shrouded by the mists of the Kuriles, and they were busy loading fuel drums. American intelligence had no knowledge of their departure. Cleverly, those ships that had been left behind had stepped up radio communications, sending a stream of false messages to be monitored by the unsuspecting American receiving sets. From all outward appearances, the carriers and the two battleships were still in the home waters of the Empire.

Of course, the other elements of Nagumo's strike force, the submarines, were well along their routes to Oahu. Even the five I-16 class midget sub carriers, proceeding via the direct route under the very noses of Johnston and Wake Islands, were having an easy, undetected voyage.

Because of radio silence, they could notify neither Yamamoto nor Nagumo, but they had seen no signs of American patrol activity.

4

The Ships Sail

BEYOND THE Kurile Islands, which lie between Hokkaido—the northern island of Japan—and Soviet Russia's Kamchatka Peninsula, lies the icy Bering Sea. The Kuriles face the cold Sea of Okhotsk. The region is icy and bleak, misty and snow covered, home of seal and walrus.

Etorofu Island is the largest of the Kuriles, and its Tankan Bay has the best deepwater anchorage. The rugged, practically uninhabitable land and continuous bad weather made it a perfect hiding place for Nagumo's ships.

While shivering sailors transferred drums of fuel oil, pilots on board the six carriers held blackboard sessions to plan tactics and went to briefings. Engine mechanics worked over the power plants of the Mitsubishi, Aichi, and Nakajima aircraft. Gunnery personnel went over and over the machine guns in the aircraft.

It was ironic that the superb Mitsubishi fighter plane had been designed, some years previously, by an Englishman named Smith. He worked for the pioneer British firm of Sopwith. In fact, the entire Japanese navy was patterned after the British fleet. Years before, England had lent its technology to the rebuilding and modernizing of the Nippon naval forces. Even more ironic, perhaps, was the fact that much of Japan's latest equipment contained steel that came from the United States.

Aboard *Akagi,* the stern, sometimes irascible Vice Admiral Nagumo fretted and awaited developments. As hours ticked away, Nagumo felt more and more that the mission was one he didn't care to undertake. If he lost the precious carriers, Japan's ability to wage war might be ended. He would sail into the very heart of the U.S. Navy in the Pacific, and he had no absolute knowledge that they wouldn't be waiting to wipe him from the face of the ocean.

On November 25, Admiral Yamamoto issued the sailing orders, and they said, in part:

1. The task force ... will leave Tankan Bay on the morning of November 26. ...
2. Upon the opening of hostilities it will attack the main force of the United States fleet in Hawaii and deal it a mortal blow. The first air raid is planned for the dawn of X-Day—exact date to be given in a later order.
3. Upon completion of the air raid ... the task force will return to Japan.
4. Should negotiations with the United States prove successful, the task force shall hold itself in readiness forthwith to return and reassemble.

The negotiations were limping along, but both nations were only playing a game. On each side, minds had already been made up.

Nomura had a Proposal B and delivered it to Secretary of State Cordell Hull on November 20. Once again, because of Purple, Hull knew what was contained in the paper before Nomura handed it to him:

Neither country will make armed advances in Southeastern Asia or the southern Pacific.

Each country will cooperate to receive commodities from the Dutch East Indies.

Each country will mutually lift the bans on assets that have been frozen, and they will resume trade relations.

The United States will provide Japan with the oil it needs.

The United States will not interfere in China.

Proposal B was an insincere, almost insolent document, entirely unacceptable to Cordell Hull and President Roosevelt. Yet diplomatic talk had to be kept alive, and Hull discussed the situation with the governments of Great Britain, Australia, the Netherlands, and China. Then he drafted a counterproposal.

Time was the big factor. Each day war did not start was a day toward the scant chance that it wouldn't start at all. So Hull asked for more time to answer Proposal B. Nomura could not grant the time on his own authority, and he sent a message to Tokyo.

The reply to the ambassador came back swiftly, and the American radio monitors plucked it from the airwaves for Purple to decode: "...if you can bring about the signing of pertinent notes, we will wait until November 29."

But the last sentence of this message to No-mura was a chilling one: "After that, things are automatically going to happen."

Nomura, it was said, did not know when or where these "things" might happen, but Kurusu, for one, seemed to have no doubt that they would happen.

At noon on November 25, which is November 26 in Japan—Yamamoto's selected date for the departure of Nagumo's ships—Cordell Hull, joined by Secretary of War Stimson and Secretary of the Navy Knox, went to the White House and met with Admiral Stark and General George Marshall before all five went in to see the president. The White House press corps reported that their "faces were grave, their moods somber."

The president said he thought the United States might be attacked as soon as the next Monday (December 1). "The Japanese are notorious for making an attack without warning," Stimson later quoted Roosevelt as saying. The Japanese had struck Russia in 1904 without any notification, and the Chinese incidents in both 1931 and 1937 (which were in fact attacks, though the Japanese preferred not to call them that) came without warning.

The meeting was adjourned, and the officials went to their respective offices. They had little to feel heartened about. In fact, on returning to his office, Secretary Stimson was handed late intelligence information that Japanese troop and supply ships were being loaded at Shanghai. Furthermore, the first elements of these Japanese naval forces were already steaming south toward Malaya, Hong Kong, and Singapore.

FAR AWAY, at 6:00 A.M. Tokyo time this November 26, as foggy darkness covered Etorofu Island, Nagumo's striking force heaved anchor. Frigid water washed down the clanking chains. Then the ships vanished like great gray ghosts into the swirling mists. At dawn the few fishermen living on the hills behind Tankan Bay looked out and saw a barren sea once again. That huge, mysterious fleet was gone!

The next day, at 5:00 P.M. Washington time, Cordell Hull gave Nomura and Kurusu the United States' answer to Japan's Proposal B. It was a long and detailed document, this Ten-Point

Memorandum, and it said, in so many words, that Japan must stop its aggression and begin a retreat in Asia.

The tiring, aging, white-maned Hull did not believe Japan would accept the proposal. To Prime Minister Tojo the memorandum meant that Japan must turn back and give up what she had gained in China and Indochina. If nothing else, such a retreat would mean a great loss of face, a loss of prestige, in Asia. That, Japan could not accept.

Knowing the contents of the Ten-Point Memorandum and Hull's pessimistic feelings about it, on November 27 the army and navy began to send out messages to military commanders in the field. Those receiving copies included General MacArthur in the Philippines, and Admiral Kimmel and General Short in Hawaii. The message began, "This dispatch is to be considered a war warning. . . ." It predicted that the Japanese might attack in the Philippines, the Thai or Kra peninsulas, or possibly Borneo, all places very far from Hawaii. Except for the Philippines, they were tied to the British, the Dutch, or the French. Britain's big naval base, Singapore, was at the foot of Malaya, the peninsula extending out from

Thailand. Even well-traveled military officers had to check their world maps to pinpoint Borneo, the island lying between the Java Sea and the South China Sea.

There were other messages tapping out on that tense day, including one to Short from the army's G-2, warning him that sabotage could be expected. He replied that he was on the alert for subversive activities and was coordinating his defenses with the navy. His mind was still completely occupied with the dangers of sabotage—and certainly not with the possibility of an outside attack on his army installations.

Short's reply to the War Department produced no reaction on the part of Secretary Stimson, General Marshall, and other high-ranking officers. They were satisfied that he had taken proper action.

In Japan, Prime Minister Tojo and his cabinet reviewed the Ten-Point Memorandum. Actually, they did not give it much thought. Tojo considered it an insult. They discussed the earnest cabled appeals of Nomura and Kurusu asking permission to continue their attempts to reach a peaceful accord with the United States.

On November 28, Nomura and Kurusu received an answer from Tokyo. Tojo informed them that the imperial government's views would be transmitted within a matter of days. Meanwhile, they must do the best they could and not give the impression that negotiations with the United States had been broken off.

At the same time, Japan's news agency, Domei, released a story for the press, giving the Japanese people the first official indications of the negotiations' outcome. The Domei story called the Ten-Point Memorandum an "ultimatum" and declared that "there is little hope of bridging the gap...."

Tokyo's leading newspaper, *Asahi Shimbun,* commented, "A showdown has come...."

For all practical purposes, negotiations had ended. Even the emperor was helpless. The next day, he summoned his *Jushin,* the elder statesmen, to the Imperial Palace. They lunched and talked. Former prime minister Konoye hoped the two powers might continue their present relationship, deadlocked but not warring; former prime minister Mitumasa Yonai was afraid Japan might lose everything because of her fears of being strangled economically. The elder statesmen listened to an analysis of the situation written by Prime Minister Tojo, Foreign Minister Togo, and others.

Of those present at this meeting, only two army generals believed that war was the single course left for Japan.

In the afternoon, the *Jushin* met with the cabinet, expressing the same fears and doubts. But General Tojo was unmoved. To accept the economic sanctions imposed by America and England, he insisted, was to die a slow death.

The *Jushin* did not know that Vice Admiral Nagumo's fleet was already on the high seas, steaming north and east. Neither did the emperor, who expressed his feelings poetically: "...why can't all men live in peace?"

However, another night was to spread across Japan before the final and formal decision to use military force was made. On December 1, the emperor agreed to a meeting of the Imperial Conference. This meeting was a last-minute review of the plans to open an Asiatic war front and strike the Hawaiian blow that would begin Japan's engagement in World War II. Germany had already agreed to support Japan and promised to declare war on the United States if Japan attacked.

These meetings—these far-reaching decisions that would eventually touch almost every human being in all parts of the world—were not even dimly suspected by the people of San Francisco or Boston, by the residents of snowy Wyoming or warm Georgia.

Throughout America now, including all the Hawaiian Islands, Christmas decorations were going up in shops and homes. They symbolized goodwill to all men.

In Honolulu, the strains of "The First Noël" and "Silent Night" floated out, accompanied by the liquid sounds of guitars.

At that moment, in that part of the world, there still was *peace on earth*.

5

"Execute the Winds" Message

ENSIGN YOSHIKAWA was very busy. Each day he observed the ships in Pearl Harbor, their arrivals and departures. On November 28, he reported to Consul Kita and then to Tokyo that the USS *Enterprise,* one of the three U.S. carriers in the Pacific, had gone to sea. Two battleships, *Oklahoma* and *Nevada,* with a pair of cruisers and twelve destroyers, also cleared the harbor entrance that morning.

Task-force commander Vice Admiral William F. "Bull" Halsey took the *Enterprise,* three heavy cruisers, and nine destroyers off to Wake Island to deliver a squadron of marine fighters. The carrier *Lexington* was scheduled to leave in a few days to drop another squadron of marine fighter planes on Midway Island. The only other "flat-top" in the Pacific was the USS *Saratoga,* now in San Diego waters for repairs. The old *Langley,* the navy's first carrier, was in the Philippines, being used as a seaplane tender instead of an attack vessel.

More than any others, the aircraft carriers were the ships that Nagumo wanted to destroy. As a pilot, he well understood the power of air warfare. Like the air admirals of the American navy, he no longer believed that battleships were the mainstays of a fleet.

So the flat-tops' movements worried him. In fact, Yoshikawa's report on the departure of *Enterprise* caused alarm on the bridge of *Akagi* as the ship plunged steadily through fog and towering seas on the northern route. He speculated as to where she was going, and why. It was something to think about as the ships proceeded toward a refueling date, a final topping of the tanks before changing course and sweeping toward Hawaii.

Below decks, pilots and crewmen in the six carriers practiced dummy bombing runs by dragging sheets beneath the aircraft. Targets had been drawn on the sheets.

Morale was high, and the pilots were eager, the samurai spirit very evident. Although America had been friendly for years, and most Japanese people seemed to admire the United States, an almost ferocious hatred was growing now in the air groups. As their hatred grew, so did their confidence.

Prime Minister Tojo convened the Imperial Conference at 2:00 P.M. on the afternoon of December 1. The meeting had been called primarily for the emperor's benefit, since in most minds the decision to wage war had already been made. There would be no turning back.

General Tojo explained why Japan must use military force. The emperor sat quietly; he did not utter a word. In the Japanese way, this silence permitted those involved to claim that the emperor had given the plans his approval.

Only one major step still had to be settled— the time that the United States would be notified of the opening of hostilities.

Both Admiral Osami Nagano, the navy chief of staff, and his assistant, Vice Admiral Seiichi Ito, had earlier demanded that the attack come as a complete surprise, without warning of any kind. They did not have too much regard for Yamamoto's daring plan, and like Vice Admiral Nagumo they feared the loss of the entire task force if the enemy had time to organize a defense.

Yamamoto and Foreign Minister Togo disagreed with the Nagano position. They believed attack without warning was uncivilized. This was not the world of 1904, when the Japanese had taken Russia by surprise. It was 1941 now, and there were rules for the conduct of war. Yamamoto insisted on some prior notification, an interval long enough for the United States to become aware that war was imminent—yet not long enough for the Americans to prepare themselves.

At this meeting of the Imperial Conference, Yamamoto's influence prevailed. Hull would be notified of the termination of negotiations, in effect a declaration of war, at 1:00 P.M., almost an hour before the first bombs would fall.

But the diplomatic game continued. Tojo stressed that the Americans must keep on believing that negotiations were still possible.

Foreign Minister Togo termed the Ten-Point Memorandum "fantastic, unrealistic, and regrettable," for the benefit of Japanese newsmen. But he issued a formal statement in softer words for Washington's benefit:

The United States does not understand the real situation in East Asia. It is trying forcibly to apply to East Asiatic countries principles and rules not adapted to the actual situation in the world, and is thereby tending to obstruct the construction of the New Order. This is regrettable.

In the late afternoon Yamamoto received his final orders: Japan, under the necessity of self-preservation, had reached a decision to declare war on the United States of America, the British Empire, and the Netherlands. At the start of the war, the commander in chief of the Combined Fleet would direct an attack on the enemy fleet in the Hawaiian area and reduce it to impotence, using the First Air Fleet as the nucleus of the attack force.

The formal phrasing of the orders really boiled down to one word: Attack. The next morning Yamamoto issued his own orders to Vice Admiral Nagumo, using the decisive, prearranged code words *Niitaka Yama Nabore!* ("Climb Mount Nitaka!")—meaning, "Attack Pearl Harbor, diplomacy has failed!"

The wind howled around Nagumo's strike force of twenty-seven ships as he received his message. For almost four days he had been battered by the weather, and if the storm kept up, his chances of refueling from the tankers were not good. Sailors had been washed overboard, and the little destroyers were taking a heavy beating from the rough seas. But the hooded skies and foul weather also hid him from observation.

After he received the *Niitaka* message, Nagumo ordered his force to darken ships and set Condition Two, a state of alert next to actual battle condition. Accordingly, the ships were blacked out, and lookout watches were increased.

By day's end, the seas began to calm, and the task force, steaming at thirteen knots, entered a fog.

DURING THIS first week in December, American intelligence experts were busy attempting to monitor every kind of Japanese radio transmission. This was being done on the U.S. mainland, in Hawaii, in the Philippines, and at every other strategic wireless tracking outpost. Radio traffic was still heavy from Japan's Inland Sea, as the ships remaining there tapped out the false messages to cover Nagumo's absence.

But at Pearl Harbor, the Pacific Fleet's intelligence officer, Lieutenant Commander Edwin

Layton, was mystified. He could not account for two entire Japanese carrier divisions, comprising four carriers and their supporting ships. No radio traffic from the four carriers had been intercepted recently. In addition, the whereabouts of several Japanese battleships puzzled him.

The Japanese trick of increasing radio traffic in the Inland Sea had obviously not been 100 percent effective.

Layton informed Admiral Kimmel. The admiral reportedly replied, "Do you mean to say that they could be rounding Diamond Head now, and you wouldn't know about it?"

Various messages being intercepted in Hawaii at that time would probably have been of great interest to Kimmel and Layton—who, however, did not know of their existence. Army Signal Corps operators picked up one transmission from Tokyo to Consul General Kita in Honolulu:

In view of the present situation, the presence in port of warships, airplane carriers, and cruisers is of utmost importance. Hereafter, to the best of your ability, let me know day by day. Wire me in each case whether or not there are any observation balloons above Pearl

Harbor, or if there are any indications that they will be sent up. Also advise me whether or not warships are provided with anti-mine nets. ["Anti-mine" nets, as the Japanese called antitorpedo nets, were made of steel, and they extended from the ship's hull to protect it from torpedo attack.]

This message was from Captain Kanji Ogawa, a key figure in Japanese naval intelligence and an expert on the American navy in particular. Ogawa had organized and administered the Japanese spy system in Hawaii.

ON WEDNESDAY, December 3, luck smiled on Vice Admiral Chuichi Nagumo. The seas were calm enough to conduct refueling operations. The ships soon had the wallowing big tankers by their sides, and fuel was pumped aboard. They steamed steadily onward.

Just as the American operators were monitoring Japanese transmissions, radiomen in Nagumo's ships were listening to Hawaii around the clock, waiting for indication of an alert, any warning that might tell them the task force had been discovered. Although no American aircraft or ships had been sighted, the strike force could easily be seen from the periscope of a patrolling submarine. Honolulu's radio stations KGU and KGMB came in clearly, but they broadcast only music and talk—nothing about an enemy fleet approaching.

In fact, Nagumo had luck that he didn't even know about. A Japanese courier plane carrying Tojo's top secret war plans to the senior Japanese general in Canton crashed in China's Waiyeung Mountains. But the Chinese communist guerrillas who found the plane could not read, and they used the war plans to light their campfires.

On Thursday, December 4, Pearl Harbor was bustling. The USS *Lexington* sailed for Midway Island with her cargo of marine fighter planes. Three heavy cruisers and five destroyers accompanied her. Carriers always had a screening force to protect them against surface or submarine action. The *Lexington* was to conduct a combined search-and-battle training exercise to the south and west of Hawaii, after delivering the marine fighters that would augment the weak Midway defenses.

Ensign Yoshikawa, ever present and always watching, duly recorded the departure of the *Lex-*

ington in a message to Tokyo. He also listed the ships that sailed with her. This message was relayed to Nagumo. Now it was apparent that there might not be any carriers in Pearl Harbor on Sunday. It was disappointing news to the Japanese.

This same day, at least two, and perhaps more, naval radio operators heard a Tokyo news transmission that ended with *Higashi no kaze ame*—"East wind, rain." The phrase was repeated twice, the signal for all Japanese embassies and consulates in the United States and England to burn secret records and codes. Next would be a full break in diplomatic relations.

The intercepted message, later to achieve a certain fame in congressional hearings as the "Winds Execute" message, was studied in Washington at the Navy Department. But those who saw it supposedly came to the conclusion that it meant attack in Manila, Hong Kong, Singapore, or the Dutch East Indies, or that it simply meant Japan would break off diplomatic relations.

Admiral Stark, Kimmel's superior, was one of those who reportedly saw the message—a stunning communication no matter what it meant. Other members of his staff also saw it, including

Rear Admiral Richmond Kelly Turner, Stark's chief of war plans. Yet Admiral Kimmel was not informed of it.

So another day and another night passed, and the sun rose on Friday, December 5.

In Washington, Purple was clacking away with the latest intercept from Tokyo. It was an order from the Japanese Foreign Office instructing most members of the embassy to leave American soil within a few days. Soon afterward, Nomura sent a cable back to Tokyo, and Purple deciphered it: "Destruction of most of the embassy codes is completed."

Whatever attention these messages drew in military intelligence and in the State Department didn't change the fact that in Hawaii, at least, Ensign Yoshikawa was taking direct action. He flew in a small rented plane for a final look at the ships in port. It rained in the morning, and the day was chill and blustery, but the visibility was good. He studied the naval base.

Pearl Harbor is like a giant, irregular mushroom, with a rather narrow neck that leads out to sea. The naval air station, Ford Island, a base both for seaplanes and for aircraft with conventional landing gear, sat in the middle of the harbor.

Along both sides of Ford Island were ship moorings; on the south side was Battleship Row.

Southward, across the channel from Ford Island, lay the naval station and the Navy Yard, with its dry docks, shops, and sheds. North of the naval station were the submarine piers and Kimmel's CINCPAC headquarters. Farther south of the naval station stood the Army Air Corps base, Hickam Field.

Ship anchorages dotted the naval base harbor, from West Loch, nearest the harbor entrance, back to the reaches of East Loch, usually a roosting ground for destroyers. There was also Middle Loch and Southeast Loch. The deepest water, of course, was around Ford Island, where the "heavies"—the battleships and the carriers—stayed. Dredges kept that water to a controlled depth of at least forty feet.

Yoshikawa had a good, long look at Pearl Harbor and Hickam Field. Then he returned to the ground again and headed for the consulate compound on Nuuanu Avenue. Soon he began drafting what would be one of his final messages from Honolulu. The message informed Tokyo of the exact number of major combatant ships in port at day's end.

Meanwhile, a wax cylinder had been turning at the Honolulu FBI office. This cylinder was recording a Japanese conversation between a person named Mori in Honolulu and a staff member of one of Tokyo's leading daily newspapers, *Yomiuri Shimbun*. For some time both the army's G-2 and the FBI had suspected that Dr. Motokazu Mori, a dentist, and his wife might be confidential agents.

Telephone lines to the Mori home on Wylie Street and to Dr. Mori's office on Nuuanu Avenue, not far from the consulate, had been tapped. Mrs. Mori was supposedly a correspondent for *Yomiuri*, reporting on the activities of the large Japanese colony in Honolulu, but today's call, which her husband took, seemed rather strange.

Yomiuri asked, "Are airplanes flying daily?"

Mori answered, "Yes, lots of them fly around."

"Are they large planes?"

"Yes, they are quite big."

"Are they flying from morning till night?"

The paper asked many questions, including some that seemed ridiculous. Others, though, inquired about searchlights and whether they were turned on when the planes flew at night, about the number of sailors around town, about the U.S. fleet, and about the weather.

Then, completely baffling, "What kind of flowers are in bloom in Hawaii at present?"

Mori answered, "Presently the flowers in bloom are fewest out of the whole year. However, the hibiscus and the poinsettia are in bloom now."

After a few more questions, the conversation went back to flowers again, and Mori said, "Japanese chrysanthemums are in full bloom here..."

The wax cylinder kept turning until the *Yomiuri* voice thanked Mori and signed off, saying, "Best regards to your wife."

The questions were hardly of the type that were usually asked a newspaper correspondent over long distance—the two had talked not only about what might be military intelligence but about flowers and even herring roe and Japanese soy sauce. A very strange conversation!

As a matter of routine, the wax cylinder was removed but not transcribed until the following morning.

6

This Means War

IN WASHINGTON, Saturday, December 6, was
only a partial day of work for many in the military establishment—even for the staffs of the
intelligence and communications offices, where
personnel were on duty around the clock. But
then no war alert, of any type, had been issued
for either the army or the navy.

So the officers, sailors, soldiers, and civilians
in the Navy Department and the War Department could look forward to going home at noon,
or by four-thirty at the latest. Christmas shopping
was much on their minds.

Two officers were not so fortunate. They were
Colonel Rufus Bratton, chief of the Far East section of G-2, Army Intelligence, and Lieutenant

Commander Alvin Kramer, in the Far East section of the Office of Naval Intelligence.

Both Bratton and Kramer had followed the Magic messages, as well as other monitored and decoded Japanese communications, for months. Lately, they had lived night and day with Magic.

Bratton had openly predicted war by November 30, but his superiors did not agree with that estimate. Thus far, they had been proven right. November 30 had come and gone, and Bratton was chided for his incorrect estimate. His "mistake" made him look not quite the expert he was supposed to be. Now his superiors would not be inclined to accept his judgment on future estimates.

Yet as this day dawned, Bratton was more than ever convinced that a Japanese attack was very near. He knew a lot about the Japanese and the way they thought. He had had duty in Japan, and he spoke the language fluently. He was the army's chief expert on Nippon.

Tall, thin Alvin Kramer was also very much a student of the Japanese, and he also spoke the language fluently. He, too, believed that war was only a matter of days, if not hours, away, but like

Bratton he had not been able to gather much support for his ideas from his superiors.

Even before Bratton and Kramer reached their offices this morning, a navy radio-monitoring station on the west coast of the United States advised Washington that it had picked up a communication from Tokyo to Ambassadors Nomura and Kurusu. Soon the message was decoded and translated:

1. The Government has deliberated deeply on the American proposal of November 26 and as a result we have drawn up a memorandum for the United States contained in my separate message #902. (It will be transmitted in English, rather than Japanese.)

2. This separate message is a very long one. I will send it in fourteen parts and I imagine you will receive it tomorrow. However, I am not sure. The situation is extremely delicate, and when you receive it I want you to please keep it secret for the time being.

3. Concerning the time of presenting this memorandum to the United States, I will

wire you in a separate message. However, I want you in the meantime to put it in nicely drafted form and make every preparation to present it to the Americans just as soon as you receive instructions.

This pilot message, telling Nomura and Kurusu how to handle the Fourteen-Part Message, which would break off diplomatic relations, was sent by Foreign Minister Togo.

Bratton correctly guessed that the Fourteen-Part Message to come would be of tremendous importance, and because of its length he requested navy help in handling it when it arrived.

At about the same time, a message was supposed to have been transmitted from the army's G-2 to General Short in Hawaii, telling him that the Japanese embassy in Washington was reported to have burned code books during the night. But there is no record of this message ever reaching Short, and there is some confusion as to whether or not it was even sent.

On the navy side, the head of the security intelligence section of Naval Communications, Commander Laurence Safford, attempted to send a message to Admiral Kimmel instructing the marine outpost on Wake Island to destroy all secret documents. Safford was worried that the documents might be captured if the Japanese landed on Wake. But his superiors thought Safford was overestimating the danger; they also disagreed with the urgency of the matter. The message was altered so it would not cause alarm, then sent by the slowest method. The top officers seemed to resist the idea that Japan might hit the mid-Pacific islands; still less did they fear for Hawaii.

On instructions from Admiral Stark, such a message did go out to Kimmel during the day. It did not mention Wake Island specifically, but it gave Kimmel authorization to have his outlying bases destroy secret and confidential documents whenever the admiral felt the need for it. Again, the communication conveyed no sense of urgency.

In the early afternoon, while awaiting copies of the Togo pilot message, the message that alerted Nomura to the upcoming Fourteen-Part Message, Colonel Bratton left his War Department office in the Munitions building to go next door to the creaking Navy Department building for a chat with Commander Arthur McCollum, head of the Far East section for Navy Intelligence.

McCollum agreed with Bratton that war was

likely to come within a few days, and they discussed Malaya and the Dutch East Indies area. Then Colonel Bratton wondered aloud about the possibility of an attack on Pearl Harbor. Commander McCollum almost scoffed at the suggestion. He pointed out that the major units of the fleet were not at Pearl Harbor. He was positive they had sailed, or were about to sail.

Oddly enough, many of the top navy officers also thought the fleet had sailed. Probably some saw the departure reports on the *Enterprise* and *Lexington.* Two battleships had steamed out the same day as *Enterprise,* but had later returned. Whatever the impressions in Washington, the battlewagons, presumed the most powerful units of the fleet, were to be found at that moment on the south side of Ford Island.

THE STATE DEPARTMENT and the White House were in a flurry of activity that day. During the late morning and early afternoon Secretary of State Hull talked frequently to both Secretary of the Navy Knox and Secretary of War Stimson. The phone calls resulted from a mid-morning dispatch from the British Admiralty reporting two Japanese task forces moving slowly toward the Kra Peninsula, past Cambodia. A total of thirty-five troop transports had been sighted in those two groups.

In his headquarters at Manila, Admiral Hart was already aware of this movement from his own sources.

Then, at the White House, on this sixth day of December, President Roosevelt made a decision. In light of the past week's events, he decided a direct appeal to Emperor Hirohito was the only course left open. The president knew the emperor had little control over the destiny of his country at that time, but there was always the chance that the saddened monarch in the Imperial Palace could somehow effect a miracle.

The second paragraph of Roosevelt's appeal began, "Only in situations of extraordinary importance to our two countries need I address Your Majesty on matters of state. I feel I should now so address you because of the deep and far-reaching emergency which appears to be in formation...."

Put in personal terms, the message was a friendly one. Roosevelt seemed to consider the movements of Japanese ships toward Indochina the basis of the dangers that existed between the two nations, and the peoples of Asia. But the cable to the emperor did not leave Washington until about nine o'clock that evening, although it was dictated to the president's secretary in late afternoon.

Then, in Tokyo, Japanese authorities held up the cable for many hours, quite probably by design.

So even that final gesture by President Roosevelt was caught in the traps of human error in Washington by its slowness of handling, and in the traps of intrigue in Tokyo. When Ambassador Grew, who was to relay it to Hirohito, finally received it, more than fifteen hours after it had been dictated, the message was worthless.

THE FOURTEEN-PART Message to Ambassadors Nomura and Kurusu began flowing into Washington after the noon hour on December 6, relayed from the Puget Sound monitoring station and picked up also by another monitor in nearby Maryland. The army had released its Purple operator for the day, and it fell on the navy's machine to decode the message.

An inexperienced officer was on duty in the navy section, and he made several mistakes in setting the proper key for the navy's Purple. The sensitive machine promptly broke down, and not until late afternoon did another, more experienced officer manage to get it working again.

A little after 7:00 P.M., the thirteenth part cleared the machine, and now the task was to type up the message neatly; it was more than three thousand words long.

At 9:00 P.M., finally, six copies of the typed message were delivered to Colonel Bratton in the Munitions building. He had been waiting for them—not exactly patiently—since noon. He was disturbed when he discovered he hadn't received the fourteenth part. Either the navy monitors had missed it, or the Japanese had not sent it. Puzzled and frustrated, Bratton decided to go home after ordering an assistant to wait for part fourteen.

He attempted to reach his boss, General Sherman Miles, to tell him of the availability of the thirteen parts, but Bratton could not locate him. He left a call for the general and then started home with his locked leather pouch containing a copy of the message. He stopped by the State Department to give the pouch to the duty officer with instructions that it was to be taken immediately to Cordell Hull at the Carlton Hotel.

At the Office of Naval Intelligence, a weary Commander Kramer gathered his six copies together. He informed McCollum and the ONI chief, Captain Theodore Wilkinson, of the general contents of the thirteen parts, and they agreed the message should be delivered to the White House and to Secretary Knox, the sooner the better.

A bit after nine, Commander Kramer's wife pulled up to the main navy building on deserted Constitution Avenue, and she and her husband drove to the White House. The president was attending a dinner party that evening, but left early, looking very solemn.

When Kramer arrived, the president was in the Oval Office with Harry Hopkins, who never seemed to be too far away from Roosevelt and was often called the "second president."

Kramer handed his pouch to Lieutenant Robert Schulz, who was on temporary duty as the assistant naval aide. The young officer took it to the Oval Office. He unlocked the pouch for the president and remained standing nearby as Roosevelt read other messages first and then finally picked up the thirteen parts.

He read the typed pages and passed them to Hopkins, who labored through them. Then Roosevelt commented, "This means war!"

He did not, however, summon his cabinet, nor did he relay his feelings of alarm to his military leaders. Perhaps he believed it meant war within a week or a month, not hours.

The thirteen parts discussed the many areas of disagreement between the two nations—stressing Japan's side of the issues, of course. The message referred to the Chinese war; to Japan's establishment of bases in Indochina; to American, British, and Dutch economic domination in Asia; and to past demands of the Japanese government.

Part ten began:

> It is impossible not to reach the conclusion that the American government desires to maintain and strengthen, in collusion with Great Britain and other powers, the dominant position it has hitherto occupied not only in China but in other areas of East Asia.

Part thirteen concluded that America, in collusion with Great Britain, Australia, the Netherlands, and China, and catering to Generalissimo

Chiang Kai-shek, was ignoring Japan's position in Asia.

The thirteen parts left little doubt as to Japan's grievances and little room for further peace negotiations.

Schulz recovered the documents, replaced them in the pouch, and left the Oval Office to return the pouch to Kramer, now waiting in the White House basement.

The next stop for Kramer was the Wardman Park Hotel, residence of Secretary Knox. Knox, too, was startled by the message. He called both Henry Stimson and Cordell Hull to arrange a ten o'clock meeting on Sunday morning, hopeful that the fourteenth part would have been transmitted by that time.

Kramer then crossed the Potomac River to Arlington, Virginia, where Captain Wilkinson lived. The army's General Miles was a guest in the Wilkinson home that night, and they discussed the message. Both viewed it as a diplomatic and not a military threat; therefore they saw no reason to awaken General Marshall at his quarters in Fort Myer, also on the Virginia side of the Potomac.

Wilkinson did reach Admiral Stark, and he in turn discussed the Tokyo memorandum with President Roosevelt. Other high-ranking officers in the navy were told of it, but on understanding that Admiral Stark knew of it, every one of them decided that the proper steps had been taken and went back to bed.

Admiral Husband Kimmel, commander in chief of the Pacific Fleet, was not informed.

It was past midnight, already December 7 in Washington, when Commander Kramer and his wife went to their own home in Arlington. Extremely weary now, Kramer retired for the night. He went to bed with the firm belief that Japan would strike within hours, probably at Singapore, plunging England into still another war.

7

Last Day of Peace: Honolulu

ON THE WINDY morning of December 6 a fire burned behind a building on Nuuanu Avenue in Honolulu. The fire was of interest to FBI observers—the building was one of the five in the Japanese consulate compound. Consul Kita's bonfire was soon reported to General Short's intelligence staff, but no one relayed this information to the general himself.

The fire was the result of the "Winds Execute" message from Tokyo, and smoke was likewise drifting up from other Japanese government offices in numerous parts of the world. All secret records and codes were being burned.

Fires of a more intense nature were licking at the boilers of Vice Admiral Nagumo's ships, now speeding toward position for the dawn launch the next morning. The supply train of tankers had turned back, its job done, and despite the mounting seas the Pearl Harbor Strike Force was approaching twenty-six knots.

At 8:00 A.M., Nagumo was handed a message from Tokyo listing the ships present at Pearl Harbor as of December 5. Nagumo scanned it, noting that the American aircraft carriers were still at sea. He wondered exactly where they were.

His orders from Yamamoto were to reverse course and flee if he was discovered before December 6, but it was now that date and he'd had no sign of discovery. The broadcasts from Honolulu continued to come in without interruption, hour after hour of music and commercials—no word of war preparations. Nor was there any indication that Ambassadors Nomura and Kurusu would score a last-minute diplomatic success. So Nagumo must press on.

If Nagumo had been able to read the morning newspaper, the *Honolulu Advertiser,* he would have learned from the headlines that America was probably going to reject Japan's demand for Indochina. In a separate article he could have read that the Japanese navy was advancing toward the south, probably toward Indochina. The newspaper made the gloomy prediction that the Nippon envoys had small chance of success with their negotiations. Yet there was nothing in the *Advertiser* to hint that within another day bombs would fall locally.

In the afternoon, Ensign Yoshikawa drafted another message for Tokyo: No barrage balloons, big sausagelike balloons that made it difficult for pilots to dive-bomb and strafe targets, could be seen around Pearl Harbor. He did not think antitorpedo nets had been placed around the battleships.

Tokyo promptly relayed the message to Nagumo.

AT ABOUT four o'clock, during the third quarter of the Shriners' football game between Willamette University and the University of Hawaii—the season's top sports event in Honolulu—Lieutenant Colonel George Bicknell, General Short's counterintelligence officer, received a rather excited phone call from FBI agent Robert Shivers.

The Mori conversation of the previous day, that baffling dialogue between Dr. Motokazu Mori and Tokyo's *Yomiuri Shimbun,* had been transcribed from the wax recording cylinder and translated. Agent Shivers had the feeling that something was going to happen.

Bicknell drove to the FBI office at Merchant and Bishop streets in Honolulu and read the long list of questions and answers. He agreed immediately with Shivers that the conversation was ominous. It was certainly a strange conversation, with those references to aircraft and searchlights. The blooming flowers? Could they be code words of some type?

In his role as a counterintelligence agent, Bicknell decided that the conversation should be made known to General Short. He called Lieutenant Colonel Kendall Fielder, Short's G-2 representative. It was after five o'clock now, and Fielder explained that both he and the general had a social engagement tonight. But Bicknell insisted the Tokyo conversation might be of utmost importance.

He went immediately to General Short's quarters at Fort Shafter, fighting through traffic from the just-finished football game.

Short read the transcription, but neither the general nor Colonel Fielder shared Bicknell's anxiety. They could not figure out what the conversation meant, and Fielder termed it silly from the

American point of view. So the general ended this impromptu meeting at Fort Shafter by suggesting to Colonel Bicknell that perhaps his alarm was not really warranted. However, they would discuss the Mori conversation further in the morning. It was then 7:30 P.M.

Short and Fielder, with their wives, went on to the social engagement at Schofield Barracks, an army installation about twenty miles from Pearl Harbor. Bicknell, understandably annoyed by their lack of interest, returned to his own home. He was unaware that the general didn't know that Kita's staff had burned secret documents.

At that moment, Admiral Kimmel was at the Halekulani Hotel on Waikiki Beach. He was attending a dinner party given by an Annapolis classmate. It had been a busy day for CINCPAC, ending at about 3:00 P.M. after a staff meeting at Kimmel's submarine base headquarters.

CINCPAC had discussed the perplexing whereabouts of the Japanese carriers and the consulate's bonfire. But attack, at least on Hawaii, had not been mentioned.

FOUR HUNDRED MILES away, in rolling seas that would make aircraft launching hazardous, and under heavy black clouds, all hands stood at attention in the ships of Vice Admiral Nagumo. It was about 9:00 P.M. The loudspeakers rang out with a message from Admiral Yamamoto: "The rise and fall of the empire depends upon this battle. Every man will do his utmost."

As the last words echoed out on *Akagi*, a battle flag broke from a halyard, flapping out in the strong wind. It was Admiral Heihachiro Togo's flag—the same flag that was run up on his command ship, *Mikasa*, thirty-six years earlier, just before his sweeping victory over the Russian fleet in the Straits of Tsushima. Hoisting it tonight was Yamamoto's idea.

Cheers roared from every ship of the strike force, and then another signal flag broke from *Akagi*'s top halyard: "Speed, twenty-six knots. Course south." The big task force wheeled and began driving across the whitecaps toward the dawn launch point 270 miles north of Oahu.

BY 9:30 P.M., Admiral Kimmel, never a party man, was back home and in bed. General Short and Colonel Fielder had left the party at Schofield Barracks and were headed back to Fort Shafter.

Kimmel and Short had scheduled their regular Sunday golf game for the morning.

By nine-thirty, Ensign Yoshikawa had sent his last message to Tokyo:

> The following ships were observed at anchor on the sixth: 9 battleships, 3 light cruisers, 3 submarines, 17 destroyers. In addition, there are 4 light cruisers and 2 destroyers lying at dock. It appears that no air reconnaissance is being conducted by the fleet air arm.

After the message was transmitted, Ensign Yoshikawa went outside—guessing, but not knowing, that the attack was not too many hours away. Neither Kita nor Yoshikawa had been informed of the exact plans. Both realized they would probably be taken into custody after the bombs fell. The ensign looked at the haze of lights from Pearl Harbor. All seemed peaceful; all seemed quiet. Then he went off to bed. It would be a restless night for Yoshikawa.

But it was definitely not bedtime for the majority of the off-duty personnel on Oahu. From Wheeler Field, with its planes parked neatly, wing tip to wing tip, and patrolled by sleepy guards against sabotage, all the way past sugarcane and pineapple fields to Pearl Harbor, the evening was a gay and noisy one.

Sailors on liberty and soldiers and marines with passes that permitted leave this night jammed downtown Honolulu, which glittered with colored yule lights. Movies were packed. Taxis were doing brisk business.

At the "O" clubs, the officers' clubs at the bases around the island, the bars were busy and dance bands played the hit songs of 1941. That wishful song "The White Cliffs of Dover"—there will be peace in England, somehow peace everywhere—was on every orchestra's request list.

At the Naval Receiving Station, in the new Bloch Recreation Center, there was even a contest going on between bands of the Pacific Fleet, a musical battle to see which ship's band was the best. It was a loud and happy time at the Bloch rec hall.

Silence did not begin to fall across the island until midnight, when the bars closed and the sounds of "Good Night, Sweetheart" drifted from a dozen places.

Offshore, only a few miles away, the long, threatening shapes of submarines were resting quietly on the surface. And waiting.

8

What Did
"One O'Clock" Mean?

THERE WAS a time difference of five and a half hours between the eastern mainland and its island possessions in Hawaii in 1941. At 7:00 A.M. in Washington, D.C., this crisp, clear Sunday morning, it was still deep night in Honolulu, with the Aloha Tower clock's hands at 1:30 A.M.

At seven o'clock in Washington, Colonel Bratton was en route to his office, as were Commander McCollum and Commander Kramer. Each man had spent a rather uneasy night, knowing that the crucial fourteenth part of the message from Tokyo was due to be sent to Nomura and Kurusu, or had already been sent. They reached their desks in the buildings on Constitution Avenue about the same time, 7:30 A.M.

Bratton needed to wait no longer. Already on

his desk, decoded by Purple and army personnel during the night, was the fourteenth part. The words did not come as a particular surprise to the colonel:

> The Japanese government regrets to have to notify hereby the American government that in view of the attitude of the American government it cannot but consider that it is impossible to reach an agreement through further negotiation.

The other thirteen parts of the message, already received of course, meant little now. In this fourteenth part the Japanese had finally made their position clear, in plain, unmistakable language. The long diplomatic road had come to an abrupt end.

Bratton immediately routed copies to General Marshall's office, to the army's G-2, and to the State Department. He also sent copies over to Commander McCollum in the Navy Department, and within minutes Commander Kramer departed for the White House with his locked leather pouch. Kramer had an extra copy to deliver to the State Department, as an added measure to ensure that this important message would reach Cordell Hull.

While the fourteenth part was being delivered, another Tokyo intercept was fed into Purple:

Will the ambassador [Nomura] please submit to the United States government (the secretary of state) our reply to the United States at 1:00 P.M., on the seventh, your time.

After deciphering part fourteen ... please destroy at once the remaining cipher machine and all machine codes. Dispose in a like manner the secret documents.

Bratton gasped. "One P.M., on the seventh, your time..." The time jumped out at him. It had to mean something! What time would that be in Manila? Two A.M., he figured quickly. What time in Hawaii? The answer was 7:30 A.M. Sunrise, or near it.

Hawaii!

Bratton knew Japanese military history. Most of their previous attacks had come at sunrise. Attacks without warning! Or with a warning so subtle that the Western mind did not comprehend it.

Bratton was frightened. He went immediately to General Marshall's office with the new intercept. But he was informed that the general was still in his residence at Fort Myer.

Bratton instantly phoned Fort Myer and was informed that General Marshall was out riding "somewhere along the Potomac." On Sunday mornings Marshall often took a canter on his favorite horse, with his dalmatian trotting faithfully behind.

In an urgent voice, Bratton told Marshall's orderly that the general must be located. Marshall had to call Bratton immediately.

At 10:00 A.M., President Roosevelt was still in bed. The fourteenth part was delivered to him there by Captain John Beardall, his naval aide. Roosevelt read it, and reportedly his only comment was, "It looks like the Japanese are going to break off negotiations." He was also informed of the one o'clock meeting between Cordell Hull and the ambassadors.

Yet, strangely, he did not confer with Hull, Secretary of War Stimson, Secretary of the Navy Knox, or either General Marshall or Admiral Stark. He spent some part of the rest of the morning taking treatment for his sinus condition.

General Marshall returned to his home at about 10:15 and called Bratton at about 10:25. He went immediately to his office, reaching it sometime around 11:00 A.M.

A bit earlier, Commander Kramer returned from his rounds to find the "One O'Clock" intercept. He, too, was alarmed and believed that the Japanese would attack somewhere at 1:00 P.M. But unlike Bratton, Kramer estimated the attack would come far out in the Pacific, perhaps in the Gulf of Siam—a blow against the British and Dutch.

He was not thinking of Pearl Harbor.

In Admiral Stark's office, a conference took place between the admiral, his top staff, and Commander McCollum. They all agreed there was something significant about the "One O'Clock" message, and it looked for a moment as if Admiral Stark would place a telephone call to Admiral Kimmel in Honolulu. But then he decided against it.

In General Marshall's office, another conference was under way. After reading the fourteen parts and learning of the last Purple decipher— the one o'clock delivery instruction—Marshall placed a call to Stark. America's two top military leaders conferred, and Marshall suggested an alert be sent to Hawaii, Panama, and the Philippines. But Stark thought that enough warnings had already gone out.

General Marshall, however, did draft a message:

> The Japanese are presenting at 1:00 P.M. Eastern Standard Time, today, what amounts to an ultimatum. Also, they are under orders to destroy their code machines immediately. Just what significance the hour set may have we do not know, but be on the alert accordingly.

This message was intended not only for Hawaii but for the army commands on the west coast of the United States, as well as in Panama and the Philippine Islands. It was 11:50 A.M. (6:20 A.M. in Honolulu) when Marshall gave the message to Colonel Bratton for transmission.

So the army, if not the navy, was going to be put on war alert.

At the Signal Corps message center, the duty officer, Colonel Edward French, checked the various methods of sending the message in order to determine which would be the quickest. For almost two hours this morning the War Department's radio circuit to the Pacific had had trouble with static. French finally decided to send the message by commercial telegram. It would be relayed by RCA Radio. Had he used the powerful Naval Radio Station at nearby Arlington, Virginia, the message would have reached Hawaii in minutes.

Over at the State Department, Secretaries Hull, Stimson, and Knox were holding the meeting scheduled the previous night. They all felt Japan was ready to attack, but they spent most of their time discussing what the United States might do if the Dutch and British were attacked.

The morning passed.

General Marshall returned to his quarters at Fort Myer; Secretary Knox met with Admirals Stark and Turner for lunch, and President Roosevelt had lunch in the Oval Office at the White House. He looked forward to working on his stamp collection in the afternoon.

The war alert from General Marshall? It was on its way to Hawaii, but it had been sent *routine* instead of *urgent*.

9

"Depth-Bombed Sub"

FIVE DARK SHAPES, long and low, moved on the surface of the waters about eight miles off Pearl Harbor this chill, windy Sunday morning, December 7. They were the First Submarine Squadron, five of the undersea craft that had sailed from Japan in November, and the time had come for their stealthy operation to begin.

At 1:00 A.M., Hawaii time, they slid beneath the choppy water, leaving only great boils and foam on the face of the ocean. No one saw them. In a few moments four of them released the midget submarines they had carried across the Pacific in big watertight tubes on the decks.

In the fifth submarine, the *I-24,* the midget craft was having compass difficulty, and twenty-three-year-old Skipper Ensign Kazuo Sakamaki and his teammate, Petty Officer Inagaki, urged the mechanic to hurry repairs. They were eager to join the attack.

Manned by volunteers—men willing to die for their country—the midgets had orders to penetrate the harbor once the aerial attack began. They had been training for months for this single mission.

The little boats looked like oversize torpedoes with conning, or control, towers attached. Forty-one feet long, each sub carried two torpedoes and despite its small size could travel 175 miles on its storage batteries. So the eight miles to the harbor entrance was no distance at all for the midgets.

A steel antisubmarine net had been strung across the entrance to Pearl Harbor and anchored on both shores with a gate in the middle. The men planned to follow incoming American ships through the gate. They would hide in the churning wakes and sneak past the steel netting, then lie on the bottom of the harbor until the airplanes began to bomb. Then they planned to surface and release their deadly torpedoes.

The plan was a startling, daring one, and even Admiral Yamamoto had serious doubts about it. Yet the spirit of the men and their willingness to go on this first of the kamikaze "suicide missions" swayed his judgment.

With Ensign Sakamaki and Petty Officer Inagaki still struggling with the faulty gyrocompass on board their midget, the other four midget subs, floating free of their mother vessel, set course for the entrance to the harbor, moving at five knots.

A bit later, Sakamaki—anointed with ceremonial perfume, wearing the samurai headband or *hashimaki*, and clad in a leather jacket and a *fundoshi*, a small garment like a pair of trunks—gave up on the balky compass and passed the word that he was now ready to be launched.

Far to the east of the submarines' thin trails of bubbles, there was other military movement in the night. Twelve U.S. Army Air Corps B-17 bombers were droning through the skies en route to Hickam Field for refueling and a rest stop after a flight from the West Coast. The big four-engined bombers were headed for the Philippines to help General MacArthur's forces there.

It was a fourteen-hour flight from California for the big planes, long and tiring. They were flying individually instead of in formation, because formation flying required more gas. Fuel was a very definite problem. To save weight, the planes had been stripped of all but essentials. Even their machine guns, protection against fighter-plane attacks, were rendered useless with heavy coats of preservative grease.

Their radios were tuned to Honolulu's station KGMB. The army had requested that the station play music throughout the night to aid in guiding the B-17s to a safe landing at Hickam Field in the morning. They would "home" in on the KGMB broadcasts.

Ironically, this same recorded music, mostly Hawaiian songs, was heard on Nagumo's carriers. They were "homing," too.

THE HOUR approached 2:00 A.M. Although most of the Pearl Harbor Strike Force pilots tried to sleep, it was a tense, restless night in the Japanese task force, and Vice Admiral Nagumo, for one, did not leave the bridge of the *Akagi*. He knew the twin-engined navy PBY flying boats on patrol could discover him at any moment. His ships were leaving long tracks of natural phosphorescence in their wakes, easily spotted from aloft. Maybe an American destroyer or a submarine routinely snooping around would see the big force.

The uninterrupted music from Honolulu was calming, though. If the Americans had been aware of Nagumo's ships, the air would be crackling with warnings, or the station would be ordered off the broadcast airwaves. But the normal programs played on, and it was now almost 4:00 A.M.—time for the aircraft crews to be awakened for launch preparations.

In the background, the wakening crews heard such soothing songs as "Sweet Leilani, Heavenly Flower."

The small U.S. minesweeper *Condor* chuffed along outside Pearl Harbor. There was always a possibility that an enemy submarine might come up and lay mines around the harbor entrance. So the *Condor*, with a sister ship, *Crossbill*, had the job of "sweeping" the waters with equipment that would catch or explode the planted mines.

Lately the men aboard the *Condor* hadn't even caught a fish, much less a mine, but at 3:42 A.M., watch officer Ensign R. C. McCloy sighted an unusual white wave off to his left, on the port side of the ship. The wave was moving, and it was less than a hundred yards away.

McCloy asked his helmsman, the man at the wheel, to look through the binoculars. They decided it was a submerged submarine, and both knew that it was not permitted around the harbor entrance. Any sub approaching Pearl Harbor must be on the surface, and all the sub skippers knew this.

A few minutes later the *Condor*'s blinker light flashed out a message to the nearby USS *Ward*, an old destroyer also on routine patrol off Pearl: "Sighted submerged submarine on westerly course, speed nine knots."

The *Ward*'s commanding officer, Lieutenant William Outerbridge, put his ship on action alert by sending all hands to general quarters—action stations—and for almost an hour he conducted a search of the area. But the midget submarine, probably sighting the *Condor*, had changed course and gone farther out to sea to await a better opportunity to move into the harbor entrance.

Lieutenant Outerbridge took the *Ward* off alert. The ship continued its search in a more leisurely and routine way. Outerbridge eventually went to his cot on the command-deck level, to be handy in case something else was sighted.

The sea plays many tricks on human eyes, and it was always very difficult to be certain that a deadly submarine had been sighted. Whales, fish, floating logs, and even tin cans have been mistaken for the undersea marauders. Many times a ship had been called to general quarters, her guns manned—to find the "sub periscope" was just a harmless tree branch. Outerbridge thought the *Condor* might have sighted just another branch.

Meanwhile, the sea gate to Pearl Harbor, the gate in the middle of the antisubmarine nets, had been opened. At a few minutes after five the *Crossbill* moved through, and just after five-thirty the *Condor* called it a night, ended her sweeping, and entered the harbor, too.

Traffic was scheduled to move out of the harbor soon, at daybreak, so it didn't make sense to the sailors manning the booms to close the gates. Opening or securing the booms usually took ten minutes.

The Japanese midget subs now had clear access to the naval base's waters if they were lucky enough to find an incoming ship and hug her wake, entering behind her.

In this black predawn, aboard Nagumo's carriers less than 250 miles from Pearl Harbor, the pilots were dressing. They had bathed the night before, and this morning, some, like Ensign Sakamaki, dabbed special perfumes on their bodies. Even the breakfast was ceremonial: They ate *sekihan,* rice boiled with tiny red beans, a dish eaten only on the highest and most solemn occasions.

The seas were still heavy; the carriers pitched and rolled as they continued southward. Aircraft already waited on the flight decks, dotted with spurts of blue exhaust as mechanics warmed up the engines. Two seaplanes had been launched from the heavy cruisers *Tone* and *Chikuma.* They were winging toward Pearl Harbor for a final reconnaissance of the American bases.

Breakfast finished, the pilots went to the briefing rooms of *Akagi, Kaga, Hiryu, Soryu, Zuikaku,* and *Shokaku.* In front of them, on blackboards, was written the latest information on the American fleet, as well as wind and weather data.

Vice Admiral Nagumo came down from the *Akagi*'s bridge to the briefing room to give the pilots a pep talk, and then he spoke privately to the flight leader, Lieutenant Commander Fuchida. Grasping Fuchida's hand, the crusty flag officer told him he had every confidence the raid would be successful.

The pilots then drank ceremonial *sake,* the traditional Japanese rice wine, and paused a moment to pray before the small Shinto shrines on board each ship. There were cries of *"banzai!"*— the Japanese warrior chant—and then the pilots ran to the flight deck and leaped into their planes.

Fuchida's aircraft, a three-seat Nakajima-97, or "Kate" to the Americans, with a bomb beneath, had red and yellow stripes on the tail. He alone was allowed to use his radio once the planes were airborne; he would direct all the other pilots on the first wave until they got over the target. The others maintained radio silence to avoid alerting the Americans. Fuchida would give the final order to attack.

Ready to man his plane, Fuchida was stopped by the chief of the aircraft maintenance crew and handed a *hashimaki,* the same type of headband that Ensign Sakamaki was wearing in the midget sub. Wearing this headband meant that the warrior was ready to die for his country. Tears in his eyes, Fuchida tied it on, and then he climbed into his cockpit.

Every crew member not on duty below was

now crowding the carriers' flight decks. Almost every eye in the task force was on the *Akagi* as she waited for the launch signals. A trail of steam rose from each flight deck, indicating the wind direction. It was an east wind, and brisk, fine for launching. But the high seas caused the carriers to pitch, creating a hazard to departing planes.

The sailors ran up flags on the *Akagi*. The flags straightened out and popped in the wind. The task force formation swung around, heading the carriers directly into the stream of the wind. The ships settled down on the new course.

Then Vice Admiral Nagumo's personal battle flag rose on the *Akagi*, joining the tatters of Admiral Togo's banner from the great victory over Russia in 1905.

On the deck of the *Akagi*, a green light made a circle in the thinning darkness as the launch officer waved the first aircraft to take off. Chocks were pulled, and full throttle was pressed. The lead aircraft trembled with power as the brakes were released.

The men's cheers were drowned out by the thunder of Lieutenant Commander Itaya's Zero fighter plane as it charged down the deck. Blue exhaust stabbed out from its manifold. As the wheels left the wooden planks the plane dipped. It seemed to hover under the bow of the ship for a moment and then gained altitude, vanishing into the gray-black predawn.

Aboard the five other carriers, it was much the same—the fighters took off first, to fly protection for the bombers and torpedo aircraft. Finally, as a bright orange sun began to peep above the horizon, Fuchida launched his plane from the *Akagi*.

The aircraft joined up in formation, and Fuchida, calling on his twenty-five years of flying experience, led them toward Pearl Harbor. The time was about 6:30 A.M. It would take them more than an hour to arrive over their target.

WHILE THE First Air Fleet was jockeying into formation to the north, the American naval supply ship *Antares* arrived off Pearl Harbor after a trip to the South Pacific island of Palmyra. She was towing a barge. The tug *Keosangua* headed out from Pearl Harbor to meet her. The antisubmarine gate had been left open for the two ships.

The *Ward* was still prowling about, half-heartedly looking for that mysterious submarine the *Condor* had reported. Then Seaman H. E.

Raenbig, at the helm of the *Ward,* saw something very curious in the wake of the *Antares.*

It was a black object, lurking in between the *Antares* and the barge she was towing. This object was also spotted by a navy PBY patrol bomber circling overhead. To Raenbig, it looked like a submarine.

He roused Lieutenant Outerbridge from his doze on the cot. Outerbridge took a look himself. Only one look was needed. He ordered the ship to general quarters. No question about it, that was a sub out there. He signaled all engines full ahead.

In the navy patrol plane above, Ensign William Tanner had an even better view of the submarine. But he thought the sub was an American vessel in distress. He dropped two smoke bombs on it, so rescuers would have an easier time spotting it.

Outerbridge wasn't thinking about rescuing anything. He was planning to attack. The little sub following the *Antares* had its conning tower about two feet out of the water. It was not like any submarine Outerbridge had ever seen. The U.S. Navy did not have midget submarines!

"Commence firing," Outerbridge ordered.

The first shot, fired at 6:45 A.M.—which became the first shot of the war between Japan and America—zoomed harmlessly over the midget sub. Gun Captain Russell Knapp's second shot smashed the sub's conning tower, and the little craft reeled as the *Ward* steamed past. The sub banged against the destroyer's hull.

Seconds later, four depth charges rolled from the stern of the old four-stacker, sending geysers into the air, smashing the sub to the bottom.

Then the PBY patrol plane, seeing the action below, joined in, and the ocean erupted again.

The sub that was following the *Antares* was definitely sunk and destroyed, but now, on the *Ward,* and up in the navy PBY, there was a lingering question: Did the submarine belong to the American Pacific Fleet?

Ensign Tanner was also having second thoughts.

But Outerbridge, a veteran officer, had no doubts about what he had done. He radioed the Fourteenth Naval District headquarters at Pearl Harbor: "Depth-bombed sub operating in defensive sea area." The time was 6:51 A.M.

After a moment's consideration, Outerbridge decided to send an even stronger message: "Attacked, fired on, depth-bombed, and sank sub-marine operating in defensive sea area."

Now, at the Fourteenth District headquarters, there should be no mistake as to what had happened off the harbor entrance.

10

Attack! Attack! Attack!

THAT "mysterious thing in the hills," the electronic device that had caused gossip back in November, was operating this morning. It was a top secret British invention called radar. Set on mobile platforms so that it could be moved from place to place, the device was a sort of electronic eye that could look far out over the seas and into the sky.

Five such radar stations were located around the island, and when working, they could pick up an aircraft 150 miles away. The unit sent out a beam, and when an object interrupted the beam a "blip," a small mark, appeared on a glass tube, or scope, rather like the later television tube.

Telephone lines ran directly from these mobile radar stations to the Combat Information

Center at Fort Shafter. When an operator saw an incoming or outgoing aircraft or ship on his radar scope, he immediately informed Fort Shafter and the target was plotted on boards. Radar tracked the target as it moved along. Experts decided whether the aircraft or ship was "friendly" or "enemy." If they thought it was the latter, they issued an alert.

The Opana mobile radar station, on a high ridge near Kahuku Point on the north end of Oahu, was always manned between 4:00 A.M. and 7:00 A.M. General Short believed this period was the most likely time for an enemy to attack.

For almost three weeks, army Privates Joseph Lockard and George Elliott, hastily trained for radar operations, but by no means experts on the amazing new apparatus, had the lonely duty at Opana. They were there to spot aircraft and report them to Fort Shafter, but everyone saw the job as training more than anything else. So far they had had no enemy sighting to report.

This morning the two men awakened at a quarter to four. They had the radar warmed up and working by 4:00 A.M. sharp. Only now, at 6:45 A.M., did they see anything on the scope. They reported several planes approaching from the northeast, more than a hundred miles out. These were probably the reconnaissance seaplanes launched from the *Tone* and the *Chikuma.*

But the duty officer in the Information Center at Fort Shafter, Lieutenant Kermit Tyler, made nothing of the report. In fact, Lockard and Elliott were advised to "secure" the set, to shut it down.

Fifteen minutes later the Information Center was practically deserted. Everyone except Tyler had gone off to breakfast. He still had one hour of duty left, and then the center would close down until the next morning. Tyler was an Army Air Corps pilot, and this radar duty was simply additional training for him. It was rather boring, too.

Back at Opana, Lockard and Elliott were waiting for the breakfast truck to come rolling up their ridge, and to while away the time they decided to keep the radar set in operation. Elliott, who had the least experience, was at the dials when a large blip showed up on the scanner. It was so large that Lockard thought the radar set must be out of order.

He sat down at the dials. No, the set seemed to be working all right, although they'd had constant trouble with it. Like any other new apparatus, especially a sensitive electronic gadget, it had occasional problems. But the system was certainly working okay now. As Lockard read off the distance and direction, Elliott plotted the blips.

The blips were 137 miles away, to the northeast, larger than any either Lockard or Elliott had ever seen on the scope. Dozens of planes!

At 7:06 A.M., an excited Private Elliott called Fort Shafter, getting through to Private McDonald, the switchboard operator. McDonald listened, scribbled down the information, and took it to Lieutenant Tyler, who was waiting only for the clock hands to settle on 8:00 A.M. so he could go home.

Tyler was not at all disturbed by the large image on Opana's scope, and McDonald called Lockard to tell him that the lieutenant wasn't concerned. "Bugs" in the equipment was the obvious answer, he thought.

The blips were bigger than ever, Lockard reported, and they were closing in rapidly. At 7:15 A.M., he estimated they were only ninety-two miles away.

Again, Private Lockard attempted to impress Lieutenant Tyler. He requested to talk personally with him. Tyler picked up the phone and listened to Lockard, but he decided the planes must be friendly. He knew the navy carriers were out on operations, and it was possible that some army aircraft were arriving, as well. KGMB had stayed on the air all night, usually an indication of an incoming overseas flight.

"Don't worry about it," Tyler finally told Lockard.

But the breakfast truck still hadn't arrived, and the two young privates continued to watch the blips as they came ever closer.

By 7:39 A.M., they were twenty-two miles from the island of Oahu.

LIEUTENANT OUTERBRIDGE, on the USS *Ward,* had sent his two messages off to the Fourteenth Naval District headquarters, but they were in code. It took a few minutes to decode them, so not until 7:12 A.M. did duty officer Lieutenant Commander Harold Kaminsky see the startling slips of paper. He immediately called Captain John Earle, chief of staff to the commander of the naval district, Admiral Claude Bloch.

Almost thirty minutes passed while Earle and Bloch conferred on this report from Outerbridge. Both officers were surprised, to put it mildly.

Depth-bombing a submarine almost on the edge of the harbor? Surprising—if not stunning—news!

There had been a number of sub sightings within the past few months, not many of them confirmed, and it wasn't clear in the minds of either Earle or Bloch that Outerbridge actually *saw* the submarine that he claimed to have sunk. They wanted positive confirmation, and so they informed Commander Kaminsky.

It was 7:40 A.M. now, only one minute after the Opana radar had established that the planes were twenty-two miles away. The phone rang in Admiral Kimmel's quarters at Makalapa, a housing area on high ground across from Pearl Harbor that afforded a good view of Battleship Row.

Kimmel was told of the *Ward*'s action, canceled his golf date with General Short, and prepared to go to his headquarters at the sub base to investigate the details of the claimed sinking.

AT ABOUT this moment, Lieutenant Commander Fuchida, leading the forty-eight Nakajima B5N1 high-level bombers—each carrying a 1,600-pound armor-piercing converted naval shell—looked down through a hole in the clouds.

He saw a long tumbling line of surf that pounded in along the north coast of Oahu. The navigation had been good. He was over Kahuku Point.

He couldn't have asked for better weather. Even the ten-knot wind was from the north, aiding him. There were heavy clouds around the mountain peaks east and west of Pearl Harbor, but the weather report indicated only scattered clouds over Pearl Harbor itself. He had been listening to station KGMB. In fact, only moments ago he had made a navigational change to home in on the broadcast beam.

Spread out in the skies around, below, and above him flew the strike force. To his right, and at a lower altitude, were Lieutenant Commander Murata and his forty Nakajima-97 (Kate) torpedo planes; to his left, Lieutenant Commander Takahashi's fifty-one Aichi dive-bombers, carrying 500-pound bombs.

Above the bombers and torpedo planes, watchful for any arising American aircraft, the forty-three Mitsubishi Zero (or Zeke) fighters were flying protection. They were ready to respond to orders from Lieutenant Commander Itaya, who'd had the honor earlier that morning of being the first pilot off the *Akagi*.

They drummed on through the broken clouds. No other aircraft flew into sight. Actually, a few civilian planes were aloft, but except for the incoming B-17 flight from California, no army aircraft were up. The marine planes were all still on the ground at Ewa Field this morning, and the few navy patrol bombers on duty were routinely scanning sea areas at various distances from Oahu.

Yet Fuchida was still not certain that the Americans were truly asleep down there and had no knowledge of his presence in the skies. The scout planes from *Tone* and *Chikuma,* whose job was to report on enemy air defense, had been silent. Nonetheless, at about 7:40 A.M., it was time to make a decision—time to deploy his aircraft. He'd been given two plans, one to activate if surprise was achieved and the other in case surprise was lost. In case of the latter, the dive-bombers and fighters would hit the airfields and antiaircraft defenses first; then the torpedo planes would come in when resistance lessened.

Fuchida believed surprise had been achieved, and he slid his cockpit canopy open. He fired a visual signal with a flare pistol—"One Black Dragon." It meant the torpedo planes would go in first and hit the major ships; then his own horizontal bombers would attack, and finally the dive-bombers. That was Genda's carefully planned tactic.

Commander Murata saw the "One Black Dragon" signal and started his torpedo group down to a lower altitude. The dive-bombers began to climb to 12,000 feet. Fuchida's own group would fly at 3,500 feet for the horizontal bomb runs. But the fighters above them did not seem to be responding to the signal. So Fuchida fired a second shot from the flare pistol.

Although Fuchida meant simply to arouse Commander Itaya and his Zeros, the dive-bomber pilots took the signal to mean "Two Black Dragons," or "Surprise is lost." Now, as the planes proceeded along the coast in a southwesterly direction, confusion reigned in the formation as both the dive-bombers and the torpedo bombers headed for a simultaneous instead of a separate attack.

Some civilians—and undoubtedly some military personnel—saw the aircraft in the sky along the coastline between Kahuku Point and Kaena Point. But though they wondered about the large numbers, they were not alarmed. They decided the army or navy must be exercising, although such activity was not usual for a Sunday. None of the planes was close enough to reveal the "red meatballs" Japanese flag insignia on their fuselages.

At 7:49 A.M., when the formation split up nearly opposite Waialua Bay, Fuchida turned to his radio operator, Warrant Officer Mizuki, and ordered the attack.

Mizuki hit his Morse code key: *"To … to … to!"* Attack! Attack! Attack!

The torpedo bombers swung inland to fly parallel to the Waianae Range en route to the naval base. The fighters and dive-bombers banked sharply across the island to hit at Wheeler Field and then Kaneohe Naval Air Station.

Fuchida continued southeast with his level bombers. They cut across land by Kaena Point and flew on to orbit off Barber's Point and await their moment of attack.

There was still no sign of opposition from the ground. No fighter planes buzzed up from Wheeler or Ewa or Ford Island, no hidden guns let loose bursts of antiaircraft fire. Fuchida was amazed. Four minutes later he ordered Mizuki to radio a signal to Vice Admiral Nagumo and the rest of the task force two hundred miles away (closer than had been originally planned): *"Tora! Tora! Tora!"* Tiger! Tiger! Tiger! The code transmission meant "Complete surprise has been achieved."

Nagumo received the news without visible emotion, but certainly there was great relief on all the carriers. Admiral Yamamoto, who was aboard the *Nagato,* in Japan's Inland Sea, also heard the signal. While monitoring the bands, the *Nagato's* radio room picked up Fuchida's message.

Like Nagumo, Admiral Yamamoto displayed no emotion but asked that the time of attack be carefully checked. Fuchida's signal meant that other Japanese attacks throughout the Pacific and the Far East would now begin. The message from Hawaii came earlier than had been planned. Fuchida was ahead of schedule.

But at 7:53 A.M., the first bomb had yet to fall; the first bullets had not sprayed out of machine guns. Fuchida's aircraft were roaring to their strike positions. Their main targets were battleships, Ford Island and its naval base, and Wheeler and Hickam Fields. Some pilots were to split off the group and hit other targets—Kaneohe Naval Air Station and the marine base at Ewa. Each pilot knew his primary targets.

Pearl Harbor, the morning of December 7, 1941

After *Pearl Harbor: Why, How, Fleet Salvage and Final Appraisal,* by Vice Admiral Homer N. Wallin. U.S. Government Printing Office, 1968.

On the American ships, it was almost time for colors, the morning flag-raising ceremony.

In Battleship Row, the USS *California* was moored by herself at the head of the row; behind her, against a dock, was the fully loaded gasoline tanker *Neosho*; then more big ones, the *Oklahoma* and the *Maryland* together; the *West Virginia* and the *Tennessee* side by side; the *Arizona* moored inside the repair ship *Vestal*; finally, by herself at the end of the row, the *Nevada*.

The ships were tied to concrete quays, huge pilings offshore from the banks of Ford Island.

Across the channel, almost directly opposite the *California,* the cruiser *Helena* was tied inboard of the old *Oglala* at the naval station's dock. The battleship *Pennsylvania* and the destroyers *Cassin* and *Downes* were in the mammoth Navy Yard drydock. At dock in Southeast Loch, opposite the sub base, sat the cruisers *New Orleans, San Francisco,* and *Honolulu.* Five subs were in port.

On the other side of Ford Island, four ships were tied to the deepwater mooring quays: the cruisers *Detroit* and *Raleigh*; the former battleship *Utah,* now a target vessel; and the seaplane tender *Tangier.*

Spread out around the harbor, in Middle Loch and East Loch, and at other anchorages, destroyers nested together with support ships.

More than ninety commissioned vessels were in the harbor, and all awaited the daily routine of colors. Then those personnel who were not on duty could relax. The next occasion of any kind was church call; after that, "chow down," which usually came between eleven-thirty and twelve o'clock.

Sundays were lazy and quiet on the ships of the Pacific Fleet.

At approximately 7:54 A.M., Admiral Kimmel, still at his quarters in Makalapa, was getting off the phone with yet another perplexing report from the destroyer *Ward*. Now she'd caught a sampan, a small fishing boat, with Japanese writing on it, in the defensive sea area.

At the same minute, 7:54 A.M., General Short was at his quarters at Fort Shafter.

It was the last minute of peace.

11

This Is No Drill!

THE ATTACKING PLANES were like maddened bees in the warm early-morning air. They buzzed over Oahu, streaking between the billows of clouds in a half dozen places. Some came through Kolekole Pass, a craggy, narrow V in a mountainous cliff of the Waianae Range, almost directly behind Wheeler Field and Schofield Barracks.

The lines of attack, swift arrows crossing the rich green fields, began to split up again. Fighters and some dive-bombers peeled off to descend on Wheeler and Schofield. Other dive-bombers drove ahead toward Kaneohe Naval Air Station, where some split off again to approach Pearl Harbor and Hickam Field.

Within minutes, attacks were being made on every major military airfield on the island. Yamamoto wanted to cripple the United States' ability to launch an air defense. Genda planned to leave the parked aircraft as blazing wrecks.

At Ford Island Naval Air Station a single plane dove toward the seaplane ramp. A black object tumbled from it, and the earth shook as the plane screamed higher skyward. On its side the bright red Japanese sun gleamed. The time was 7:55 A.M.

Commander Logan Ramsey, on duty in the Ford operations office, had been busy directing additional aerial help to the *Ward* for submarine search. He heard and felt the jar of the explosion and then saw the plane. He gasped. "It's a Jap!"

Commander Takahashi guided his planes over Hickam Field, where they began to peel off toward the runways where the army aircraft sat side by side in neat rows. General Short's exaggerated precautions against sabotage, helped along by directives from Washington, were about to blow up—almost in his face. Booming explosions sounded at Hickam, and black, oily smoke thrust up into the sky.

General Short heard the explosions, but he thought the navy was having a battle practice. He went outside his quarters at Fort Shafter and saw smoke to the west. It didn't occur to him that the smoke was from enemy bombing and strafing.

In these first moments of the attack, only two people on the soil of Oahu understood completely what was happening—Consul General Nagao Kita and Ensign Takeo Yoshikawa. Later, Yoshikawa was to say that he had "strange feelings" when he heard the noise and saw the smoke.

At 7:56 A.M., enemy aircraft were sighted heading toward the northwest side of Ford Island, toward that line of ships headed by the seaplane tender *Tangier.* A few seconds passed, and then torpedoes slammed into the *Raleigh* and *Utah.* This attack seemed incredible. Most of the high-ranking officers in the U.S. Navy had thought the waters of Pearl Harbor were too shallow for torpedo attacks. Another myth—like the myth of distance—ended with a fiery roar.

Men aboard the ships on Battleship Row heard the explosions from the other side of the island and were baffled. Some saw the aircraft far away, but they assumed army or navy pilots were practicing combat tactics. Yet the action was strange for a Sunday morning, always a rest day.

A single Kate dashed across Ford Island, unleashing its torpedo toward the naval station's docks and the cruiser *Helena,* tethered inside the aged minelayer *Oglala.* Red fire burst amidships on the *Helena.* Time: 7:57 A.M.

Some slowly, some immediately, but all in amazement, the men finally understood they were under enemy attack. This was no practice! At 7:58 A.M., Rear Admiral Patrick Bellinger, commanding the land-based air arm, issued the first shattering signal to all ships in the harbor: *AIR RAID ON PEARL HARBOR! THIS IS NO DRILL!*

At 8:00 A.M., the breathtaking official CINC-PAC confirmation message went out to all naval commands around the world.

But the attack encompassed much more than Pearl Harbor. At Kaneohe, machine guns chattered as Val dive-bombers zoomed in, spraying fire-producing tracer bullets that could be visually traced through the air for more accuracy in bombing. In less than a minute, thirty-three of Kaneohe's patrol planes were afire. At Ewa Marine Corps Air Station, west of Pearl Harbor, forty-seven of Colonel Claude Larkin's forty-eight planes went up in flames and smoke as twenty-one Japanese raiders attacked.

More of Murata's torpedo planes went after the big ships. They thundered across Southeast

Loch, so low over the water that their propellers churned up whitecaps. They aimed for the massive battlewagons moored at the concrete quays.

On the *Nevada* a band was playing the national anthem for morning colors. Musicians on the exposed afterdeck calmly kept blowing their horns, following the leader's baton, in a stunning demonstration of both shock and long training. Machine-gun bullets tacked across the deck from a Kate that had already thrown its torpedo at the *Arizona*. But not until the last note of "The Star-Spangled Banner" was played did the musicians run for cover.

General quarters, the call to arms, sounded repeatedly on all the ships in Pearl Harbor. Frantic voices convinced the men that the raid was real, not some drill by crazy pilots. Whining aircraft, ear-shattering explosions, and now the screams of wounded men were beginning to communicate more than the urgent voices on the loudspeakers.

The *Oklahoma* was hit, then the *West Virginia*. Two torpedoes smashed into the *Arizona*. The *California* was also hit with a pair of them.

A MONITORING radio operator at the Mare Island Naval Station in San Francisco heard the first incredulous Pearl Harbor broadcast ordered by Rear Admiral Bellinger, meant only for ships in that area. He relayed it to Naval Communications in Washington, and an excited radioman called Admiral Leigh Noyes, the top communications officer.

Noyes, too, was stunned, but he didn't wait for confirmation. He ran straight to Admiral Stark's office. But the admiral had already gone for the day. Noyes then went directly to Secretary Knox's office. Knox read the message and blurted out, "My God, this can't be true! This must mean the Philippines." He thought a mistake had been made.

Knox called the White House and repeated the message to President Roosevelt, who was lunching with Harry Hopkins in the Oval Office. Later there would be different reports as to how the president reacted, but the most reliable one, from Hopkins, was that Roosevelt said he thought the news was "probably true."

Roosevelt phoned Stimson first, and then at 2:05 P.M., he called Secretary of State Cordell Hull to inform him of the attack. At that moment, Ambassadors Nomura and Kurusu were being ushered into the waiting room outside Hull's office.

Roosevelt dictated a statement for release to the press before resuming his lunch.

Various accounts later indicated the president remained cool and calm throughout. Hopkins's diary revealed that the president seemed to be "thankful" that the "matter was out of his hands." The enemy had chosen to strike first, and now the United States could retaliate with a clear conscience. Also, the United States could now wage war against Germany and Italy. No longer would the nation be isolationist; no longer would Roosevelt have to keep his campaign promise not to send American boys to fight on foreign soil.

Cordell Hull's first thought was to refuse to see the Japanese envoys, but on the chance that the Hawaii report was false, he decided to observe the usual amenities. But he made them wait fifteen minutes.

At 2:20 P.M., Washington time, Hull requested Nomura and Kurusu to enter his office. He did not ask them to be seated. Handing Hull the termination of talks note, Nomura said he'd been instructed to deliver the message at 1:00 P.M. and apologized for the delay, without explanation. Hull asked Nomura why he had been instructed to deliver the message about the break in relations at one o'clock, but he already knew the answer: time. The Japanese hadn't wanted to give America time to prepare for an attack.

The Japanese ambassador began to explain that there were difficulties in recording the message. Hull interrupted him in cold fury. He did not use diplomacy in his icy reaction to the sneak bombings, and he told them that their Fourteen-Part Message was full of lies and distortions. He signaled them out of the office. They left with bowed heads.

Not until the ambassadors met newspapermen in the corridor did they learn their country had attacked the United States.

Five minutes earlier the president's announcement of the attack had gone out to the news services, and at this moment America's radio stations were informing a shocked and stunned people. It was to be a moment that almost everyone over the age of six would remember for the rest of their lives.

At first the announcement was met with disbelief. No one could believe that the "little brown people" from Asia had done this. Then the country grew angry.

In Tokyo it was December 8, of course, and the Japanese people were equally stunned when the Imperial Rescript, the message from the Emperor, was read:

> We, by grace of Heaven, Emperor of Japan, seated on the Throne of a line unbroken for ages eternal, enjoin upon ye, Our loyal and brave subjects:
>
> We hereby declare war on the United States of America, and the British Empire. . . .

Antiaircraft fire was finally reaching up into the Hawaiian skies. It had taken about five minutes for the Americans to gather their senses and begin manning guns. Puffs from exploding shells dotted the air. From ships and shore batteries, every available and undamaged gun was getting into action.

The *Nevada*'s mast-top machine guns probably downed the first enemy aircraft. The plane splashed into the water. But its mission had already been completed. A torpedo plunged into the port bow of the battleship and exploded.

A second torpedo hit the *Oklahoma*. Darkness settled in the spaces below decks throughout the ship. Her generators had come off the line, and even the emergency lights were blown out. Three more torpedoes slammed into her port side, ripping it open on the oily waters of the harbor.

The *West Virginia* took another torpedo, and then, at 8:05 A.M., the *California* was hit from the water. Seconds later, she shuddered from another torpedo impact.

The deadly torpedo plane runs, led by Murata and Lieutenant Goto, were almost over. Lieutenant Commander Fuchida now began his phase of the attack with the high-level bombers. He set a course toward the *Nevada*, which was already wreathed in smoke. Ack-ack—antiaircraft fire—burst in the sky around the Kate bombers.

Water was pouring in aboard the *Oklahoma, West Virginia,* and *California.* Many men—engine-room personnel and ammunition handlers—were below decks on the ships. They heard the rumbles from above and felt the hammerlike blows of concussion through the steel skin of the hulls. Acrid, choking smoke curled down through the passageways and vent systems. Gagging fumes swept into the steel mazes of corridors sectioned off with watertight doors.

The *West Virginia* settled to the bottom of the harbor. She was the first ship to sink.

Above the harbor, bombs were spilling from Fuchida's high-level planes. One sailor described them as black snowflakes. The little repair ship *Vestal,* tied outside *Arizona,* took a bomb that had been aimed at the *Arizona.* It ripped out part of her bottom. Then two more bombs found the *Arizona.*

The *Oklahoma* was mortally wounded. Slowly, the proud battleship rolled over. It was such a slow roll that men first standing topside walked along the belly of the hull and found themselves standing on her wet bottom. Her mast and superstructure pushed into the mud. Some sailors jumped into the water, which was covered with oil that burned in many places. The *Oklahoma* was gone at 8:08 A.M.

Inside her, men screamed and panicked as water began to fill her compartments. Only pockets of air were left. The men swam and clawed in a world of darkness in which decks lay where overheads were supposed to be. Trapped inside her hull, they had no sense of direction. More than four hundred men died inside the *Oklahoma.*

12

The *Arizona* Dies

AT ABOUT 8:11 A.M., the *Arizona* lit with a searing flash as one of Fuchida's high-level bombers made a lucky hit, blowing up the ship's forward powder magazines and boilers. Fuchida's own plane rocked in the concussion as a ball of flame and smoke shot up into the sky over Battleship Row.

In one devastating split second, more than a thousand of the *Arizona*'s men were killed. The explosion's shock wave crossed the harbor, carrying a blast of such power that it swept men off the decks of the *Vestal, Nevada,* and *West Virginia.*

Rear Admiral Isaac Kidd and Captain Franklin Van Valkenburg, on *Arizona*'s bridge to direct defense, were instantly killed. When the smoke cleared a bit, there was not one sign of life on her shattered, charred, and burning decks.

About this time, Admiral Kimmel, already professionally ruined and facing further disgrace, reached his headquarters. He was far too late to do anything but hear and watch the disaster unfold. He could only hope that the casualties wouldn't be too high. The defensive battle was up to the men on the guns, and he could do nothing personally to aid them. And he could only have his men search for the enemy if he had any aircraft still undamaged—not a very likely prospect.

Bombs kept falling. Two hit the *Maryland*; and the USS *Tennessee,* moored inboard of the now sunken *West Virginia,* staggered as three more crashed into her decks.

Across the channel from Battleship Row, at the naval station's dock, the *Helena* was fighting to stay afloat. Alongside her, the *Oglala* was sinking, but not from a direct hit. The impact of the torpedo that struck the *Helena* had opened the *Oglala*'s ancient seams, and now she was as full of holes as a sieve.

On the other side of Ford Island, the bulky old target ship *Utah,* struck on the first wave of torpedo bombers, was listing heavily. Water lapped along her port side, almost at her main deck. The *Raleigh,* astern of her, also had a port list, and water had penetrated her boiler rooms.

The devastated *Arizona* was starting to show some signs of life. Men, some burned critically, most dazed and in shock, began to crawl out of twisted hatches and smashed gun turrets. There were not many of them, but a few made it aboard the wreckage of the *Vestal,* still laced to the destroyed battleship.

The *Vestal*'s skipper, Commander Cassin Young, had been blown into the fiery water. He swam back to his ship and clambered aboard. He was determined to save her, if possible. He ordered his men to chop the lines to the *Arizona.* He hailed a passing navy tug and prepared to have the *Vestal* towed to an anchorage on the other side of the harbor.

Another ship was already under way with guns fully manned, leaving behind the flames and smoke of Pearl Harbor. She was the USS *Helm,* the only vessel on the move when the first bomb fell. Now she was standing out to sea at twenty-seven knots, ready to take on anything that might come over the horizon.

It was 8:17 A.M. when she cleared the harbor

entrance. Immediately the *Helm* spotted one of the midget submarines about a thousand yards away. The nose of the little craft seemed to be up on a coral bank near the entrance buoys. The destroyer's guns opened up, but the midget slid off the coral reef unharmed. It submerged as the *Helm* radioed, "Small Jap submarine trying to penetrate harbor."

While the *Helm* was engaging the midget sub, the B-17s from California—the flight destined for the Philippines—were attempting to land at any field that looked halfway clear. As early as 8:00 A.M., they began their approaches to Oahu.

They'd been up for almost fourteen hours, and all were running low on gas, having flown to their extreme range. In fact, Lieutenant Barthlemes, skipper of one of the four-engined bombers, had thoughts of ditching his aircraft because of fuel shortage. Then he saw a group of planes out there with him. An escort, he thought. Yet, on closer look, the "escort" had red circles painted on the fuselages.

Major Truman Landon, also flying with the B-17s, had seen nine planes earlier. He only discovered they were enemy when one fired a machine-gun burst at his plane. Now, at 8:20

A.M., he landed at Hickam with three Japanese fighters on his tail. One B-17 landed with its after section burning. Several others picked small airfields that did not seem to be under attack.

Pilots off the American carrier *Enterprise* were not quite so fortunate. She had launched eighteen aircraft at 6:15 A.M. while the big flat-top was about two hundred miles away from Oahu, returning from her delivery trip to Wake Island. The planes were to scout ahead of the *Enterprise* and then land at Ford Island.

None of the pilots was aware of the scale of the attack until about 8:00 A.M., when they converged on Oahu. Five planes had been shot down, by either Japanese aircraft or antiaircraft fire from the ground. Three pilots had been killed. The other planes crash-landed or made it into Ford or Ewa, dodging fire from the U.S. Navy.

Even civilian planes had become entangled with the Japanese. Three small aircraft managed to come face-to-face with one or another enemy groups, and two of them caught Japanese bullets.

LIEUTENANT COMMANDER Fuchida's mission was now nearing its end. But a second wave of Japanese planes, 170 of them under Lieutenant

Commander Shigekazu Shimazaki, were boring toward Kahuku Point. They came in to blast at whatever ships were still floating. Later they would hammer away again at Ford Island and Hickam Field.

At about 8:25 A.M., after a final hit on the *California,* Fuchida's group began to head north. The commander himself decided to stay around and take photographs of the damage, then watch Shimazaki's planes make their attack. He still saw no air opposition from the Americans. He climbed to fifteen thousand feet.

Though for the past few minutes the main action had been around Pearl Harbor and Hickam Field, dive-bombers now hit Kaneohe again and Zeros struck at Ewa, Bellows Field, and even little Haleiwa Field—a field scarcely noticeable from the air until two B-17s made emergency landings there.

Then, a little past 8:30 A.M., the enemy seemed to vanish from the skies over Oahu. They left behind coils of black smoke and flames arising from the naval base and airfields.

The enemy hadn't vanished from the waters, though. At this very moment a Japanese midget sub was coming in for a torpedo attack. She moved up toward the west side of Ford Island. The USS *Breese,* a destroyer-minelayer, spotted the sub first. Then personnel aboard the USS *Curtiss* and the USS *Medusa* saw her, too.

Heading down the west channel was the destroyer USS *Monaghan.* All three ships warned the *Monaghan*—she was practically bow-on to the tiny undersea craft. The *Curtiss* fired several shots into the conning tower, and the *Monaghan* opened up at point-blank range as the sub fired its two torpedoes.

One torpedo streaked by the *Curtiss,* and the other missed the *Monaghan.* Both hit the Ford Island shore and exploded. As the *Monaghan* tried to ram, her bow glanced off the sub's conning tower. Slewing around, the midget banged against *Monaghan's* hull and rolled off in her wake as depth charges, set for shallow explosion, ignited. They crushed the little sub instantly.

Cheers rang out, as they had when the *Nevada* gunners got the torpedo plane. It was a small victory on this day of defeat, but a victory nonetheless.

The *Monaghan* steamed on out to sea.

So far, the midget subs had yet to score. But in one of them, at least, the men were still trying. Despite their compass troubles, and having survived one depth-charging already, Ensign Sakamaki and Petty Officer Inagaki were again moving toward the Pearl Harbor entrance, determined to destroy a ship.

13

The Second Wave

A SHORT LULL came between attacks—at most, ten minutes when the skies were clear of enemy aircraft—and somehow Pearl Harbor began to recover. There were signs of it everywhere. Men waited at the ready by their guns for the enemy to return.

The *Nevada* was trying to get under way; preparations were being made to move the sinking *Oglala* from the *Helena*'s side. The *Vestal* was nearing a safer anchorage at Aiea. There was still chaos, still havoc; men were still being pulled from the burning, debris-littered waters—but the mood had changed. It was now an angry fight back.

Over in the Navy Yard, Captain Charles Cooke of the USS *Pennsylvania,* which was under repair and sitting in dry dock, ordered the dock gates to be partially opened. Behind him, perched on chocks, were the destroyers *Cassin* and *Downes*. If the dry dock was suddenly ruptured, his big *Pennsylvania* couldn't help but crush the small destroyers in the flood of harbor waters. Meanwhile they sat ready, guns manned.

The most amazing recovery was the USS *Nevada*'s. Torpedoed and bombed in the first wave of attack, she was almost ready to sail again. At sea, at least, she could maneuver instead of staying a sitting duck on Battleship Row.

Perhaps most astonished of all were the *Nevada*'s own men. They'd always been told it took at least two hours to get up enough steam to power her engine turbines. Now, in just forty-five minutes, that steam was up. In the past she had always needed four tugs to help her sail or dock. Now she was getting under way without any assistance.

What's more, neither her captain nor her executive officer, the number two in command, was aboard. The daring decision to run from Battleship Row had been made by a reserve officer, Lieutenant Commander Francis Thomas. Normally he served as *Nevada's* damage-control officer, in charge of directing emergency repairs.

On the bridge with Thomas stood a cool, steady veteran of ship handling, Chief Quartermaster Robert Sedberry. But Sedberry had never faced a task like this, threading the behemoth downstream under almost certain enemy attack.

The *Nevada* cast off, partially hidden by the coiling black smoke over Battleship Row. At about 8:40 A.M., she moved slowly and steadily past the twisted *Arizona*. Again, cheers sounded from other ships, and from the oil-stained, half-naked survivors standing along the shore of Ford Island. The Stars and Stripes fluttered from her stern. Guns aboard her pointed skyward. The *Nevada* was suddenly a symbol of defiance.

The Americans desperately needed such a symbol. A moment later, the enemy roared in again. Fifty-four high-level Kate bombers, eighty Val dive-bombers, and thirty-six Zero fighters came in this second wave, led by Commander Shimazaki.

The high-level Kates had the first mission, going in to drop bombs on the *Tennessee* and the *West Virginia*. Six planes took part in the first attack run, and then a group of nine planes started their runs across the Navy Yard toward Battleship Row. A third group of nine planes began to concentrate on the big dry dock holding the *Pennsylvania* and the destroyers *Cassin* and *Downes*.

Guns boomed out from every sector of Pearl Harbor, from the destroyer nests in the far reaches to the Navy Yard dry docks. The sky was peppered with black bursts of shell fire.

Fuchida's planes had run into very little ack-ack. It was a different story now. Gun barrels became so hot that paint peeled off them. The defense grew furious. In the heat of it, some shells landed in Honolulu, causing civilian casualties and minor damage.

On the cruiser *New Orleans,* which had been undergoing minor overhaul at the naval station berths facing Southeast Loch, electric power from shore had been disrupted and ammunition had to be passed hand to hand instead of on mechanical lifts. Then a legend was born: Chaplain Howell Forgy, unable to participate in the fighting because he was a minister, stood on the deck to encourage the ammunition passers. Slapping their sweaty backs, he shouted, "Praise the Lord, and pass the ammunition!" (Later it was revealed that these words—popularized in a hit war song—were not exactly what he said. But they are a true indication of the spirit that was there.)

The enemy aircraft sighted the *Nevada,* now clearing Battleship Row, and swarmed over to her. The *Nevada'*s guns sent up a barrage of steel, and she was almost hidden from both air and shore view by the smoke from her barrels.

One bomb hit her, then another. Flames and flying metal covered her superstructure. A third bomb slammed into her on the starboard side. She shuddered, but she kept moving. An estimated thirty bombers were now concentrating on the *Nevada.* Near-misses sent spouts of water into the air around her as Sedberry weaved her past a dredge pipeline extending halfway into the channel.

The Japanese pilots saw a chance to sink her in the channel, perhaps blocking the harbor for months to come. On shore, senior officers watching her escape through binoculars anticipated this strategy.

Semaphore flags broke out from the Fourteenth Naval District signal tower: *Keep clear of the channel!*

If Thomas and Sedberry couldn't use the

channel, their gallant voyage was over. The *Nevada* couldn't go to sea.

At about 9:00 A.M., Thomas ordered all engines stopped, and Sedberry swung her bow toward Hospital Point, nosing into the mud. The anchor was dropped, and *Nevada*'s short run to open ocean ended. Taking water, her bridge and superstructure afire, the *Nevada*'s guns were still firing as a final bomb exploded near her bow.

Shimazaki's aircraft then turned to targets that had been all but ignored during the *Nevada*'s sprint. Bombs began to fall on the *Pennsylvania, Downes,* and *Cassin.* The dry dock almost flooded when the *Pennsylvania* took her first hit shortly after nine. While she was the real target, the destroyers took most of the near misses. In a moment both were burning stem to stern. The *Pennsylvania* shook again after a direct hit.

At 9:12 A.M., the destroyer *Shaw,* in the floating dry dock nearby, took a bomb and blazed up. The seaplane tender *Curtiss,* anchored off Pearl City, was next to be plastered; then the cruiser *Honolulu,* at Southeast Loch.

The *Shaw*'s fire had reached her forward magazines, and at 9:30 A.M., the whole blackened sky over the Navy Yard turned red as the destroyer exploded. The mushroom of the fireball was streaked red and white as shells flew up and exploded. One shell crossed the channel to fall on Ford Island.

At 9:37 A.M., a massive explosion shattered the *Cassin's* hull, and she rolled over onto the already stricken *Downes*. It was the final big explosion of the morning.

While the ships had again been the principal targets for Lieutenant Commander Shimazaki's crack pilots, Japanese aircraft had also been putting in appearances over Hickam, Ford Island, and Wheeler. The Zero fighter cover strafed Hickam and Kaneohe as well.

But this time opposition flew in the air. What the American force lacked in size it made up in courage. When group leader Lieutenant Sakamaki's planes swept through Kolekole Pass to strafe Wheeler Field, U.S. Army Air Corps Lieutenants George Welch and Kenneth Taylor had piled into a car for a dash to Haleiwa Field, a small auxiliary strip on the northwest coast. Their P-40 fighter aircraft were parked there. They called ahead to have crewmen ram in belts of ammunition for their machine guns. The aircraft were already gassed up.

At about 8:30, Welch and Taylor took off to hunt for the enemy. They flew to Barber's Point. By that time Fuchida's planes were finishing up their attacks over Pearl and Hickam and heading north again.

So Welch and Taylor flew back to Wheeler for more ammunition. They were off the ground at about 9:00 A.M., airborne at almost the same time nine Japanese strafers came to pay a final visit to the field.

Within a minute they had downed two enemy planes. Heading for Ewa, where dive-bombers were operating, they got four more. After Taylor's P-40 was hit with machine-gun fire, forcing him to earth, Welch managed to shoot down another Val.

Although there had been earlier attempts to muster fighters from Wheeler, and some later attempts, during Shimazaki's second wave, to send them up from Bellows, only Taylor and Welch were credited with air kills this Sunday.

At about 9:45 A.M., Fuchida watched as the last of Shimazaki's planes disappeared toward the north. With the gas level in his Kate, he could stay around a bit longer to make some final observations for reporting to Vice Admiral Nagumo.

Fuchida was confident that most of the heavy ships in Pearl Harbor had been sunk or severely damaged. He knew practically all the aircraft on Oahu had been destroyed. Yet some targets were still untouched. Although he did not know his own losses, he felt they were not great. (Actually, he had lost three Zero fighters, a dive-bomber, and five torpedo planes. Shimazaki's losses, due to increased antiaircraft fire and the P-40 action of Welch and Taylor, were larger: six fighters and fourteen dive-bombers.)

By now, the Japanese carriers had moved to within 190 miles of Pearl Harbor to recover aircraft, and at about 10:00 A.M., the first of Fuchida's early attack groups began arriving. Many of the fighters were low on gas. As soon as they landed, those not severely damaged were refueled and rearmed for the possibility of a third strike.

Three hundred and twenty-four planes returned from both waves. Twenty-nine had been lost, with a loss of fifty-five personnel.

Fuchida stayed on, above Oahu, until shortly after 10:00 A.M. Then he set course back for the carriers, landing after 11:00 A.M. He reported immediately to Vice Admiral Nagumo, to whom he listed the damage he believed had been inflicted on the American fleet. Then he urged another attack.

Commander Genda was opposed. He did not believe a third attack was worth the risk. Anti-aircraft opposition would be even greater next time. Furthermore, the American carriers were somewhere at sea, and Genda had no desire to engage them in battle. Hitting them in the confines of Pearl Harbor would be one thing, a duel with them on the high seas another. Why risk it? Then, too, radio interceptions indicated there were still American bombers on Oahu that could be launched.

Nagumo listened to reports from the other flight commanders. When Rear Admiral Ryuno-suke Kusaka, his chief of staff, sided with Genda in opposing a third wave, Nagumo made his decision. At 1:30 P.M., the admiral signaled to the task force to retire at top speed to the north.

This decision did not surprise Yamamoto, still on board the *Nagato* in the Inland Sea. In fact, he had predicted it only moments before. Both Nagumo and Kusaka had originally opposed the raid because of its risks, and now, after apparent success, their natural reaction was to retire, not stage another raid.

When Fuchida departed from the skies over Oahu, the only Japanese combatants still left operating were beneath the sea. Some submarines were still in the vicinity, having seen no action. They were due for an interesting day. The U.S. destroyers *Dale, Blue, Aylwin, Henley,* and *Phelp* were now at sea hunting for signs of the raiders.

The cruisers *St. Louis, Detroit,* and *Phoenix* were also under way, ready to engage if any Japanese ships could be sighted.

In their midget craft, Ensign Sakamaki and Petty Officer Inagaki continued a day of floundering. Fumes in the drifting submarine knocked them unconscious. Finally they ran aground during the night, far away from Pearl Harbor. At dawn the next day, they abandoned the little craft. Inagaki drowned, but Sakamaki made it to the beach near Bellows Field. He was the first Japanese prisoner of war taken by the United States.

14

"A Date Which Will
Live in Infamy"

AT 10:00 A.M., no one in Pearl Harbor, or anywhere else on Oahu, knew the enemy was retreating. In fact, they awaited another attack. Rumors quickly spread, some saying that the Japanese had troop transports off Barber's Point; one radio broadcast said Japanese troops had already landed. False reports came in all day. Paratroopers were supposed to be dropping, enemy battleships had been sighted, Japanese saboteurs were at work.

While all this was going on, men were still being picked out of the oily harbor waters. Ambulances rushed to hospitals with the wounded; boats crept alongside the mercy ship *Solace* with burned and wounded. Officers and men caught on shore when the attack started rushed back to their ships by any means of transportation they could get. Some had no ships to go to, and they joined in with rescue or salvage work.

The *Nevada* was pulled off the mud at Hospital Point at about 10:00 and beached on Waipio Point, across the channel. With her nose on the beach, the Japanese could not possibly sink her to block the harbor entrance.

At about the same time, the old *Oglala* gave up and rolled onto its side. "Abandon ship," called men on the *West Virginia.* There was nothing more they could do. The *California* was abandoned at 10:02 A.M., but less than fifteen minutes later Captain Bunkley recalled the crew to fight fires and save the ship.

Over on the *Utah,* which lay on her side, there were tappings from the hull. The sounds meant only one thing—men were still trapped inside her. Even as the second wave of Japanese planes gained altitude to the north, *Utah* survivors clambered back onto the slippery steel. Then sailors from the *Raleigh* and the *Tangier* arrived with cutting equipment.

It was the same on the *Oklahoma,* whose bottom lay to the sky. Navy Yard workmen joined with sailors to open holes. They listened to the tapping, located its source, and then tapped back. Blue arcs of acetylene torches sliced at the hull. But the men soon found that the gas torches ate up oxygen inside the ship. They switched to pneumatic equipment, driven by compressed air. Thirty-six hours later, when all the taps had been investigated, thirty-two of the *Oklahoma*'s men had been saved from certain death.

Three men were trapped deep inside the *West Virginia*. Long after the fires were put out on her decks and in her compartments, they were known to be alive. They were tapping, yet no one could reach them. Not until Christmas Eve were all hopes of saving them abandoned.

Two men trapped in the *California* had better luck. They were brought out at 3:00 P.M.

All over the island—at Wheeler, Ewa, Hickam, Kaneohe, Bellows, and Schofield Barracks—the immediate task was to get medical aid for the wounded and injured, put out the fires, clear away debris, and prepare to fight again. Troops were moving to bolster defenses; guns were resupplied with ammunition. The *Pennsylvania* pointed her heavy batteries toward the harbor entrance in case the Japanese returned by sea.

If Premier Tojo had expected the Americans

to give up—if he thought their will to fight had been broken by the surprise raids—he might have been disheartened to see what occurred on Oahu.

Through the movement of troops, past road-blocks, and through the general confusion, a young Japanese named Tadeo Fuchikama was riding an Indian motorcycle on his rounds, delivering RCA cables. He had a number to deliver, and although he knew the Japanese had attacked, the cables must be distributed as on any other day. He had been on his route since shortly after 8:00 A.M.

One cable was addressed to the commanding general at headquarters, Fort Shafter. Fuchikama, noting that it had not been marked urgent or given any other priority, had placed it in his pouch for routine handling. The cable had arrived in Honolulu at 7:33 A.M., more than twenty minutes before the first bomb fell.

Yet it was well after 11:00 A.M., after Fuchikama had delivered practically all the other cables, that he arrived at Fort Shafter. At approximately 3:00 P.M., the cable reached General Short. He read it, and then, without comment, ordered it relayed to Admiral Kimmel.

This message from General Marshall, the last-minute "war warning" to Hawaii, was late—tragically late.

Admiral Kimmel read it and then tossed it into a wastebasket. General Marshall's mishandled warning wasn't of the slightest interest anymore.

At 11:27 A.M., four army B-26 bombers went airborne to search for the enemy carriers. They went north, but not very far, and they found no trace of the Japanese fleet. A few minutes after noon, nine of the *Enterprise*'s undamaged aircraft were launched to search the north. They flew out about two hundred miles, but Nagumo had already vanished into the gray mists.

As the *Enterprise*'s aircraft lifted off from Ford Island, the pilots could see the devastation all over. Smoke still rose from the battered airfields, though the fires on the runways, in the hangars, and in the barracks had been extinguished. Battleship Row was blanketed in thick smoke, and the oil-fed flames on the *Arizona* would continue to burn for several days.

Lost were the battleships *Arizona* and *Oklahoma,* the target ship *Utah,* the destroyers *Cassin* and *Downes.* The *West Virginia* and the *California* were sunk, and the *Nevada* had been beached to keep it from sinking.

The battleships *Tennessee, Maryland,* and *Pennsylvania* were damaged, as were the cruisers *Helena, Honolulu,* and *Raleigh,* the destroyer *Shaw,* the seaplane tender *Curtiss,* and the repair ship *Vestal.* But all except the *Arizona, Oklahoma, Utah, Cassin,* and *Downes* would rejoin the fleet after urgent repair work. Three of the damaged battleships would put out to sea in less than two weeks.

Destroyed were 96 army aircraft and 92 navy and marine aircraft. Another 159 had been damaged.

Worst of all was the human cost. A total of 2,403 people lay dead, of whom 68 were civilians. Another 1,178 sailors, soldiers, and civilians had been wounded or injured.

But Pearl Harbor was only a part of Japan's strategy to conquer Asia and turn the Pacific into a Nipponese stronghold. Radio reports of attack were coming in from Hong Kong, from Thailand, and from the Malay Peninsula. Japan had struck on a line that stretched from the Gulf of Siam to Hawaii. Manila had been bombed. Soon

Midway, Wake, and Guam Islands would be under attack.

Japan launched her war on a wide front. She was confident that she could achieve her aims in all of Asia as well as the Pacific, now that the U.S. fleet in Hawaii was disabled. As news of the Pearl Harbor destruction was announced, there was great rejoicing in Tokyo.

The Japanese had not thought too much about America's industrial might or her ability to come back from early defeat and wage war. In fact, in the hours following announcement of the attack, few Japanese seemed to consider the possibility that the Pacific Fleet might well be rebuilt, strengthened, and set to sail again.

About eighteen hours after the *Enterprise's* planes took off in their futile attempt to find the enemy task force, President Roosevelt stood before a joint session of Congress to ask for a formal declaration of war against the Japanese Empire.

He began, "Yesterday, December 7, a date which will live in infamy, the United States of America was suddenly and deliberately attacked..." Then he called for a declaration of war for this "unprovoked and dastardly attack." As one, the nation's representatives rose to their feet, applauding and cheering.

Congress responded to his request in the affirmative. War was also declared on Germany and Italy, the Axis partners of Japan. The United States entered World War II.

The people of Japan became aware of the attack on the morning of December 8 through their radios and newspapers, reacting "first, with great surprise, then with great joy," reported the Tokyo *Asahi.*

The press of Japan was government-controlled and for months had been telling the people that the Americans were "soft and decadent," that they "lacked fighting spirit." Therefore, the immediate reactions were ones of confidence in the Imperial armies and navy. The navy had struck boldly at the U.S. military heart in the Pacific, so there was cause to rejoice.

Although the Americans were outraged at the "sneak attack," the Japanese had been fighting their wars this way for centuries, both at home and abroad. Surprise was a basic element of war, and no tears were shed in Tokyo the morning of December 8.

15

The Heroes
and the Scapegoats

NOT UNTIL AFTER the battle was over, after the guns were stilled, did stories of heroism become known. Even then, countless deeds of individual courage and self-sacrifice were never told. Surely there were heroic moments among those trapped below decks in the *Arizona,* the *Oklahoma,* and the *Utah*—split seconds of gallantry that will remain forever unknown.

But as the hours passed, as the combat-weary survivors exchanged experiences and told of what they had seen and heard, the stories ebbed and flowed. Since the beginning of mankind, after any conflict such stories are told and retold. This is how legends are born.

Pearl Harbor had its legendary figures, as the Alamo had its Davy Crockett and Jim Bowie. The

Pearl Harbor legend embodies some of the spirit of Captain Lawrence of USS *Chesapeake* in the War of 1812. Dying, he called out, "Don't give up the ship!"

Aviation Chief Ordnanceman John Finn was on the ramps at Kaneohe Naval Air Station as the first wave of attackers roared in. Picking up a loaded machine gun, Finn raced across the ramp to mount it on a stand.

Bullets laced the earth near him and wing guns peppered the parked aircraft as he began to fire back. Alone, out on the exposed ramp, Finn had no protection from the strafing planes, yet his gun roared on even after he was wounded.

Finn's citation for the Medal of Honor, the nation's highest military award, told the story:

Although painfully wounded many times, he continued to man his gun and to return the enemy fire vigorously, and with telling effect throughout the enemy strafing and bombing attack, and with complete disregard to his own personal safety. It was only after specific orders that he was persuaded to leave his post to seek medical attention. Following first aid treatment, although obviously suffering much pain and moving with great difficulty, he returned to his squadron area and actively supervised the rearming of returning planes. His extraordinary heroism and conduct in this action are considered to be in accord with the highest traditions of the Naval Service.

Ensign Herbert Jones, while assisting on an ammunition-passing detail for the topside guns, was mortally wounded when a Japanese bomb exploded deep in the *California*'s hull. His wounded mates attempted to carry him out, but he ordered, "Leave me alone. I'm done for. Get out of here before the magazines go off."

Also on the *California,* Machinist's Mate Robert R. Scott was manning the compressors that supplied the topside guns with blasts of cleaning air after each round was fired. When a torpedo ruptured the hull, letting oil and water in, Scott shouted, "This is my station. I'll stay here and give them air as long as the guns are going."

Scott slammed the steel door to prevent water from flooding the entire ship. He kept the compressors going until they were completely underwater. He died beside them.

When the *Nevada* was ready to cast off her lines and dash for the open sea, Chief Boatswain Edwin Hill climbed down to the quay and cut her loose. Then he dove into the water and swam to catch up with her. Thirty minutes later, after she grounded at Hospital Point, Hill was laboring to drop her anchor when a bomb exploded off her bow. He was blown overboard and killed instantly.

Another veteran chief petty officer, Peter Tomich of the *Utah,* calmly went about his work in the engineering spaces as the ship capsized. First he made certain that all personnel in the boiler room had cleared out, and then he secured the boilers so they wouldn't explode, adding further damage to the ship. He gave the *Utah* his life.

In the same vessel Fireman Second Class John Vaessen remained at his post. He kept the lights going until the ship's last second, so that men below decks could find their way out. After the ship rolled over, Vaessen took a flashlight and a wrench and found his way to the dynamo room. He knew the general location of a manhole leading to the ship's double bottom. Soon Vaessen was tapping on the steel with his wrench. Sailors cut a hole from the outside, and he crawled to safety.

Doris Miller was a huge and powerful mess steward in the *West Virginia*. As he was a man of color, he had been automatically assigned to mess duties. When the *West Virginia* was struck, Miller helped carry his mortally wounded commanding officer, Captain Mervyn Bennion, to shelter. Then Miller manned a machine gun. Trained for kitchen work and serving, Miller had no experience in gunnery. But he found the trigger and blazed away, laying down a harassing fire.

Miller's action proved, once again, that heroism is a matter of individual courage and has nothing to do with race or color. He later gave his life in a carrier battle. Because of men like him, before the war was over the navy began to change its policy of automatically designating black sailors as mess stewards.

Miller was awarded the Navy Cross for his performance at Pearl Harbor. Captain Bennion, who requested reports on the action until his last breath, concerned only for his ship, received the Medal of Honor posthumously.

As the *Oklahoma* capsized, Catholic chaplain Aloysius Schmitt helped four men escape through a porthole. But there wasn't time to save his own life. Chief Watertender Francis Day assisted fifteen men to safety through a submerged porthole; he, too, sacrificed himself. Ensign Francis Flaherty and Seaman James Ward helped fellow crew members escape from one of the *Oklahoma*'s big gun turrets on Pearl's murky bottom. But the two men did not have the same luck.

Perhaps the story of Marine Sergeant Tom Hailey best demonstrates the determination of the men of Pearl Harbor. Captain of the *Oklahoma*'s number ten broadside five-inch gun, Hailey was in his bunk when the first torpedo struck. Before he could reach his gun the ship capsized, and Hailey dove into the water, swimming to the *Maryland*.

When he climbed aboard the *Maryland,* he saw an antiaircraft gun not completely manned, rounded up a crew, and began firing. A bomb blast scattered Hailey's crew; then smoke and fire made it impossible to operate the gun. So the sergeant dove into the harbor again.

Reporting to the air station, he volunteered his services for whatever tasks were needed. Within a few minutes Hailey was seated in an amphibious aircraft, an old Springfield rifle in his hands. For the next five hours he flew as a lookout while the pilot searched for the Japanese fleet.

A total of fourteen officers and enlisted men received the Medal of Honor; fifty-two were awarded the Navy Cross; four received Silver Stars; and four the Navy and Marine Corps Medal.

Not all the heroes of Pearl Harbor were military personnel. Crane operator George Walters, perched high in his cab above the dry dock where the *Pennsylvania* sat, became so enraged at the attack that he attempted to fight the enemy aircraft with his crane, swinging the big hook back and forth to spoil the runs of the dive-bombers and fighters.

Civilian machinist Henry Danner became an ammunition passer on the *Pennsylvania*. Other civilians helped fill ammunition belts, fight fires, clear up bomb damage, and assist in harbor rescues.

Undoubtedly, many acts of gallantry, both military and civilian, went unrecognized.

SOME MEN in Washington and in Hawaii, at the highest levels of government and in the highest ranks of the military, had made tragic, costly, almost unbelievable mistakes. People in lesser positions and of lesser ranks also contributed to the disaster and defeat at Pearl Harbor.

Admiral Kimmel and General Short were relieved of their duties in Hawaii. Admiral Stark was sent on to other duties, as were several other high-ranking officers in Washington. But the blame for Pearl Harbor cannot fall solely on Kimmel and Short. Many people, from President Roosevelt on down, can be accused of bad judgment and gross negligence.

Several congressional committees held lengthy hearings determining that many more than Kimmel and Short had been negligent. But to this day a number of questions concerning Pearl Harbor, and particularly White House involvements, have not been answered. They may never be. Certain documents simply "disappeared." For example, the crucial "Execute the Winds" message vanished from the files.

At the time of the hearings and later, members of Congress, military writers, and columnists voiced an opinion that Kimmel and Short were merely the scapegoats of Pearl Harbor, the men who were forced to take more than their share of the blame for the disaster. Kimmel, bitter to the day of his death, in turn placed a major share of the blame on Admiral Stark.

President Roosevelt's personal involvement

has long been a matter of sharp and divided opinion. There were, and are, people who feel he might have prevented the surprise element of the attack by making certain his military commanders in the field knew of the events Magic was decoding. Harsher judgment says he welcomed the attack because it permitted entry into World War II, a step that even his most ardent critics acknowledged as inevitable.

Roosevelt's defenders, who are in the political majority, claim he had no more idea that the Japanese would strike Pearl Harbor than did Kimmel or Short. If anything, they maintain, he was a victim of lack of information and good judgment from his subordinates.

In testimony before the Joint Congressional Committee in January 1946, Admiral Kimmel said,

Assuming that for the first time on December 5 I had all the important information then available in the Navy Department, it is my conviction that I would have gone to sea with the fleet, including the carrier *Lexington,* and arranged a rendezvous at sea with Halsey's carrier force, and been in good position to intercept the Japanese attack.

... Even on the morning of December 7, four or five hours before the attack, had the Navy Department for the first time seen fit to send me all this significant information, and the additional fact that 1:00 P.M., Washington time, had been fixed for the delivery of the Japanese ultimatum to the United States, my light forces could have moved out of Pearl Harbor, all ships in the harbor would have been at general quarters, and all resources of the fleet in instant readiness to repel an attack...

Answering the same committee, General Short said,

I do not feel that I have been treated fairly, or with justice, by the War Department. I was singled out as an example, as the scapegoat, for the disaster. My relatively small part in the transaction was not explained to the American people until this Joint Congressional Committee forced the revelation of the facts. I fully appreciate the desire of the War Department to preserve the secrecy of the source of the so-called "Magic," but I am sure that could have been done without any attempt to deceive the public by a false pretense that my judgment had been the sole factor causing the failure of the Army to fulfill its mission of defending the Navy at Pearl Harbor. I am sure that an honest confession by the War Department General Staff of their failure to anticipate the surprise raid would have been understood by the public, in the long run, and even at the time. Instead, they "passed the buck" to me, and I have kept my silence until the opportunity of this public forum was presented to me...

It was a rather pathetic summary—words for history—but also words for thought for those who would administer the nation's defenses in the future. By the time of the hearings in 1946, the war with Japan had been won. She had surrendered after atom bomb attacks on two of her islands.

Actually, Japan fought a losing battle for years before the nuclear blasts at Nagasaki and Hiroshima. In June 1942, the tide of battle turned at Midway Island, when Vice Admiral Nagumo's carrier forces were routed. The *Soryu,* the *Akagi,* the *Kaga,* and the *Hiryu,* ships that had raided Pearl Harbor, were destroyed. Yamamoto's once proud force never recovered.

The Pearl Harbor raid obviously did not achieve for Japan what she had hoped. History has assessed it as a classic military blunder. Even regarded tactically, it proved to be a blunder—the Japanese did not destroy the ship-repair facilities at the naval base, the huge oil storage tanks, the ammunition magazines, or the submarine base. The submarines went out to sink enemy ships by the dozen. The carriers, at sea, were untouched.

Within six months, the Pacific Fleet was stronger and larger than it had been when Commander Fuchida victoriously signaled, *"Tora! Tora! Tora!"* It grew to gigantic proportions and eventually sank almost every fighting ship in the Imperial Fleet.

As the events at Fortress Alamo in 1836 and the sinking of the USS *Maine* in Havana in 1898 had rallied the American people with cries of "Remember the Alamo," and "Remember the *Maine,*" the slogan "Remember Pearl Harbor" was to serve the American nation as a call to arms, and finally, to victory.

Key Figures in
the Story of Pearl Harbor

Generalissimo Chiang Kai-shek: leader of the Chinese
military forces in the war with Japan at the time
of the attack on Pearl Harbor and later president
of the national government of China.

Commander Mitsuo Fuchida: led the air attack against
Pearl Harbor, the Japanese losing only 29 planes
out of 353 launched.

Commander Minoru Genda: the man primarily responsible for formulating and executing the detailed plans for the Japanese air strike on Pearl
Harbor.

Joseph C. Grew: U.S. ambassador to Japan.

Hirohito: emperor of Japan.

Cordell Hull: U.S. secretary of state.

Admiral Husband Kimmel: commander in chief of the
U.S. Navy's Pacific Fleet and the highest-ranking
naval officer in Hawaii at the time of the attack.

Nagao Kita: Japanese consul general in Honolulu.

Frank Knox: U.S. secretary of the navy.

Saburo Kurusu: Japanese ambassador to Washington.

General George C. Marshall: chief of staff of the U.S. Army during World War II, the highest-ranking army officer.

Admiral Osami Nagano: chief of staff of the Imperial Japanese Navy, the highest-ranking naval officer.

Vice Admiral Chuichi Nagumo: commander of the Japanese task force that attacked Pearl Harbor.

Admiral Kichisaburo Nomura: Japanese ambassador to Washington.

Franklin D. Roosevelt: president of the United States.

Lieutenant General Walter Short: chief U.S. Army commander in Hawaii at the time of the attack.

Admiral Harold Stark: chief of naval operations, the highest position in the U.S. Navy.

Henry Stimson: U.S. secretary of war.

General Hideki Tojo: Japan's minister of war, who in 1941 became prime minister.

Admiral Isoroku Yamamoto: commander in chief of the Combined Fleet of the Imperial Japanese Navy and the man who conceived and directed the surprise attack on Pearl Harbor.

Takeo Yoshikawa: ensign in the Imperial Japanese Navy and an important spy, responsible for providing Tokyo with information about American military installations in Hawaii.

Bibliography

Allen, Gwenfread. *Hawaii's War Years, 1941–1945.* Honolulu: University of Hawaii Press, 1945.

Bateson, Charles. *War with Japan: A Concise History.* East Lansing: Michigan State University Press, 1968.

Beasley, W. G. *The Modern History of Japan.* New York: Frederick A. Praeger, 1963.

Browne, Courtney. *Tojo, the Last Banzai.* New York: Holt, Rinehart, and Winston, 1967.

Davis, Burke. *Get Yamamoto.* New York: Random House, 1969.

Davis, Forest. *How War Came.* New York: Simon & Schuster, 1942.

Farago, Ladislas. *The Broken Seal.* New York: Random House, 1967.

Feis, Herbert. *The Road to Pearl Harbor.* Princeton, N. J.: Princeton University Press, 1950.

Flower, Desmond, and Reeves, James, eds. *The Taste of Courage: The War, 1939–1945.* New York: Harper & Brothers, 1960.

Hashimoto, Mochitsura. *Sunk.* New York: Henry Holt & Co., 1954.

Hoehling, A. A. *The Week Before Pearl Harbor.* New York: W. W. Norton & Co., 1963.

Karig, Commander Walter, USNR, and Kelly, Lieutenant Welbourn, USNR. *Battle Report, Pearl Harbor to Coral Sea.* New York: Farrar & Rinehart, Inc., 1944.

Kimmel, Admiral Husband E. *Admiral Kimmel's Story.* Chicago: Henry Regnery Co., 1955.

Lord, Walter. *Day of Infamy.* New York: Henry Holt & Co., 1957.

Millis, Walter. *This Is Pearl.* New York: William Morrow & Co., 1947.

Morgenstern, George. *Pearl Harbor, the Story of the Secret War.* New York: The Devin-Adair Co., 1947.

Morison, Rear Admiral Samuel Eliot. *History of United States Naval Operations in World War II.* Vol. 3, *The Rising Sun in the Pacific.* Boston: Little, Brown & Co., 1961.

Pearl Harbor Attack. Hearings before the Joint Committee on the Investigation of the Pearl Harbor Attack, Congress of the United States, 79th Congress. Vols. 1–11. Washington, D.C.: Government Printing Office, 1946.

Potter, John Deane. *Yamamoto.* New York: Paperback Library, 1967.

Smith, S. E. *The United States Navy in World War II.* New York: William Morrow & Co., 1966.

Theobald, Rear Admiral Robert A. *The Final Secret of Pearl.* New York: The Devin-Adair Co., 1954.

Toland, John. *But Not in Shame.* New York: Random House, 1961.

Trefousse, Hans Louis, ed. *What Happened at Pearl Harbor: Documents Pertaining to the Japanese Attack of December 7, 1941, and Its Background.* New York: Twayne Publishers, 1958.

Author's Note

MUCH ADDITIONAL DATA was obtained from magazines and news clippings as the result of research during a year's association with the filming of *Tora! Tora! Tora!*, the Japanese-American production about the raid on Pearl Harbor. Talks with Minoru Genda and Mitsuo Fuchida added perspective. Time spent at Battleship Row, Ford Island, Wheeler Field, and other installations, as well as flights over several of the attack routes, provided a fresh insight into the events. Time spent in Japan during the filming of Japanese sequences in Tokyo, Kyoto, and Kyushu also provided valuable insight as the re-created characters of Yamamoto, Genda, Fuchida, and Prince Konoye came alive. Walking the decks of the reconstructed *Nagato* and *Akagi* on Kyushu, and watching rebuilt Zeros, Kates, and Vals attack Battleship Row helped me re-enter history as it happened.

ACCLAIMED AUTHOR THEODORE TAYLOR was born in North Carolina and began writing at the age of thirteen, covering high school sports for a local newspaper. Before turning to writing full time, he was, among other things, a prizefighter's manager, a merchant seaman, a movie publicist, and a documentary filmmaker. The author of many books for young people, he is known for fast-paced, exciting adventure novels, including *Sniper*, the bestseller *The Cay*, and *The Weirdo*, an Edgar Allan Poe Award winner. While *Air Raid—Pearl Harbor!* is a work of nonfiction, it proves that real history is as compelling as any novel. Mr. Taylor was also involved with the production of *Tora! Tora! Tora!*, a film about the air raid at Pearl Harbor. He lives near the ocean in Laguna Beach, California.

*Have you read these
Great Episodes?*

———

SHERRY GARLAND
In the Shadow of the Alamo
Indio

KRISTIANA GREGORY
Earthquake at Dawn
Jenny of the Tetons
The Legend of Jimmy Spoon

LEN HILTS
*Quanah Parker: Warrior for Freedom,
Ambassador for Peace*

DOROTHEA JENSEN
The Riddle of Penncroft Farm

JACKIE FRENCH KOLLER
The Primrose Way

CAROLYN MEYER
*Where the Broken Heart Still Beats:
The Story of Cynthia Ann Parker*

SEYMOUR REIT

*Behind Rebel Lines: The Incredible Story of
Emma Edmonds, Civil War Spy*

*Guns for General Washington: A Story of
the American Revolution*

ANN RINALDI

An Acquaintance with Darkness

*A Break with Charity:
A Story about the Salem Witch Trials*

*Cast Two Shadows:
The American Revolution in the South*

*The Coffin Quilt: The Feud between
the Hatfields and the McCoys*

*The Fifth of March:
A Story of the Boston Massacre*

*Finishing Becca: A Story about
Peggy Shippen and Benedict Arnold*

*Hang a Thousand Trees with Ribbons:
The Story of Phillis Wheatley*

*A Ride into Morning:
The Story of Tempe Wick*

The Secret of Sarah Revere

The Staircase

ROLAND SMITH

*The Captain's Dog:
My Journey with the Lewis
and Clark Tribe*